200 Devo

The Wonderful Names of Our Wonderful Lord

Praying

the

Names

of God

LEANNE BLACKMORE

BARBOUR BOOKS
An Imprint of Barbour Publishing, Inc.

Print ISBN 978-1-63409-809-0

eBook Editions:
Adobe Digital Edition (.epub) 978-1-68322-082-4
Kindle and MobiPocket Edition (.prc) 978-1-68322-083-1

Published by Barbour Books, an imprint of Barbour Publishing, Inc., P.O. Box 719, Uhrichsville, Ohio 44683, www.barbourbooks.com

Our mission is to publish and distribute inspirational products offering exceptional value and biblical encouragement to the masses.

Member of the
Evangelical Christian
Publishers Association

Printed in the United States of America.

INTRODUCTION

Believe it or not, I was praying—praying that I would be a better pray-er—when I got the call.

For years I've pored over the Word, prepared lessons, taught Bible classes, and even written Bible study books. But my prayer life has always felt borderline anemic. I talked with God, asked for His guidance, presented requests to Him, and occasionally got serious and fasted. Yet the depth of my conversations seemed limited. . .my focus, shallow.

Several years ago, I led a class through the Hebrew names of God in the Old Testament. Our key verse came from Proverbs 18:10 (ESV), "The name of the LORD is a strong tower; the righteous man runs into it and is safe." It was a rich study, opening new facets in my relationship with the Lord. Learning names like Jehovah-Jireh (Our Provider), El Elyon (God Most High), and Adonai (Lord, Master) allowed me to approach God in a whole new way and run to Him to find safety and security.

The desire to tap into that type of fresh insight again prompted me to pray for my prayer life. It wasn't long after I began praying to be a better pray-er when Annie, a former Bible student, contacted me. "Remember that series you taught about the Hebrew names of God?"

"I sure do! Why? What's up?"

"Well," Annie continued, "our company wondered if you would be interested in writing a prayer devotional on the names of God. I know you focused on a few specific names when you taught, but we'd like to use a classic book entitled *The Wonderful Names of Our Wonderful Lord* as a springboard for this project. What do you think?"

She shared a few more details so I could get a better handle on the idea and asked again, "So would you be willing to write this for us?"

Realizing God might be up to something (isn't He always?), I wanted to shout out, *"Yes!"* However, I thought I should sound like I had a bit more spiritual maturity and wisdom, so I told Annie I'd pray about it and get back with her. After hanging up, I began laughing and crying at the same time. *God, You certainly know how to answer prayers above and beyond what we ask or imagine, don't You?*

Let me be honest, what started as a fresh and invigorating exercise soon became one of the most challenging spiritual journeys I've traveled. Why? Because prayer is personal. Baring my heart and soul made me vulnerable and catapulted me out of my comfort zone. And prayer is emotional. Tapping into old wounds and celebrating new victories forced me to ride a veritable roller coaster of feelings. But prayer is powerful. I found that expressing and requesting and complaining and confessing didn't necessarily move God, but He did move me—drawing me into closer alignment with His will and His ways. He moved me to fulfill the purpose for which He created me—to know Him and to make Him known!

I hope that in reading these prayers, you, too, will be moved. Moved to:

> praise God (through *adoration*)
> acknowledge your sin (through *confession*)

show appreciation for who He is and what He
has done (through *thanksgiving*)
make your requests known to our heavenly Father
(through *supplication*)

My goal was to write prayers that were specific to my life, yet general enough that you could insert your own personal story/concerns. You'll find some variety in style—prose, poetry, quotes directly from the Word, as well as paraphrasing. I've used a variety of Bible versions, too—some formal, some informal. Hopefully, the sum total of these efforts will be an added impetus for deeper conversations between you and God. I'm certain that like me, you will be amazed at the plethora of God's names found in the pages of scripture. Before this project, I thought knowing a few names like Provider, God Most High, and Master invigorated my prayer life. Little did I know a Nail Fastened in a Sure Place, Hiding Place from the Wind, and Chiefest among Ten Thousand would be names I could run to for refuge and safety, too.

So…believe it or not, I was praying—and God knocked my socks off by answering with two hundred prayers of His own! Now, through these two hundred prayers, I've asked the Lord to knock your socks off, too!

LeAnne

Contents

ADORATION

. . .because there is no god like our God

*"And there is no other god besides me, a righteous
God and a Savior; there is none besides me."*
ISAIAH 45:21 ESV

The Almighty (El Shaddai)

—⧉—

When Abram was ninety-nine years old, the LORD appeared to
him and said, "I am El-Shaddai—'God Almighty.'
Serve me faithfully and live a blameless life."
Genesis 17:1 NLT

God, You promised an old man and woman they would have a son, saying, "Is anything too difficult for the LORD?" (Genesis 18:14 NASB). And You kept that promise when they were one hundred years old and seventy-five years old, respectively—proving that *nothing* is too difficult for You!

I pray today that I will keep the same question in mind, knowing the answer will always be a resounding *"No!"*

Is it too difficult for You to bring life out of death? No!

Is it too difficult for You to calm my storm? Absolutely not.

Is it too difficult for You to provide resources when there seems to be nothing to draw from? Nope!

It's funny, God—I can almost hear You saying, "Go ahead, ask another one!" because it's clear this question becomes rhetorical when referencing You, the Almighty.

El Shaddai, I praise You for powerfully fulfilling every one of Your promises—because nothing is too difficult for You! Amen.

Altogether Lovely

∞

His mouth is sweetness itself; he is altogether lovely.
Song of Songs 5:16 niv

God, if I open my eyes and take time to look around, I see beauty everywhere—the colors of the sky, the changing seasons, the birds out my back window. If I slow my pace long enough to see the people coming and going, I notice beauty there, too—the variety of skin tones, hair textures, and personality traits is endless! I'm surrounded by glimpses of Your glory!

Lord, help me take off my blinders so I can behold Your beauty today. Let me not be so caught up in the daily grind that I miss Your magnificence. You are engaging. You are captivating. You are altogether lovely, and I love You. Amen.

The Amen

For all of God's promises have been fulfilled in Christ with
a resounding "Yes!" And through Christ, our "Amen"
(which means "Yes") ascends to God for his glory.
2 CORINTHIANS 1:20 NLT

Father, You are a God of promises. You operate in a realm of covenant.

You promised a serpent crusher would come (Genesis 3:15).

You promised all the nations of the earth would be blessed through Abraham's seed (Genesis 12:1–3).

You promised the death angel would bypass those households covered by the blood of the Passover lamb (Exodus 12:13).

You promised those bitten by the fiery serpents in the wilderness that if they looked to the bronze serpent on the pole, they would be healed (Numbers 21:9).

You promised that by Christ's wounds, we would be healed (Isaiah 53:5).

And You promised peace, love, forgiveness, eternal life, strength, Your presence, and so much more. In the economy of promises fulfilled, Your record is unbeatable! And it's because of Jesus.

He is Your "Yes!" He is Your "So be it!" He is Your "Amen!" He reflects Your glory!

I praise the name of Jesus—the Amen!

THE BABE

*"You will find a Babe wrapped in swaddling cloths,
lying in a manger."*
LUKE 2:12 NKJV

Babe in a manger—
Divinity took on flesh.
Hope was born that day.

Babe in a manger, thank You for Your humble beginnings. Right from the start You painted a picture of hope—focusing Your infinite power and grandeur on the downtrodden and broken, the lost and hurting. In surrendering Yourself in helplessness, You showed us the way to the Father. Your love is overwhelming, Lord! I bow my knee to You, for You alone are worthy! Amen.

Blessed and Only Potentate

⚬⚬⚬

[Jesus] is the blessed and only Potentate,
the King of kings and Lord of lords.
1 Timothy 6:15 NKJV

O Mighty One, Blessed and Only Potentate, King of kings and Lord of lords, to You we ascribe honor! To You we ascribe power! You alone are limitless, and no one can dispute Your authority. Your ultimate authority will be made manifest when You appear and gather Your followers who are ready to receive the promised prize. Though some may mock You now, and others deny, on that day *every* knee will bow and *every* tongue confess that You are Lord, to the glory of God the Father.

Now to Him who is able to keep me from falling, and to present me before His glorious presence without fault and with great joy—to the only God, my Savior, Jesus Christ—be glory, and majesty, and power, and authority before all times both now and forevermore (Jude 1:24–25)!

A Branch Out of His Roots

<hr>

And there shall come forth a rod out of the stem of Jesse,
and a Branch shall grow out of his roots.
Isaiah 11:1 KJV

Heavenly Father, so many miracles attest to the deity of Jesus, but the fulfilled prophecies always amaze me! "The past events have indeed happened. Now I declare new events; I announce them to you before they occur" (Isaiah 42:9 HCSB). You announced hundreds of events before they occurred—why do so many people miss this? Jesus—born of a virgin, born in Bethlehem, presented with gifts, anointed by the Spirit, had a ministry of healing, taught in parables, was crucified, dead, and buried, resurrected from the dead after three days—all these events You announced beforehand!

Out of the nations scattered over the earth, out of the line of kings who long had ceased to reign, there would come a prophet—a Branch Out of His Roots. And He came. You have told us that this Branch, Jesus Christ, will just as surely come again to reign once more over Israel, and through Israel, over all the earth. And He will.

Lord, I stand amazed! Lord, You are amazing! Amen.

CLUSTER OF HENNA BLOSSOMS

My beloved is to me a cluster of henna blossoms
from the vineyards of En Gedi.
SONG OF SONGS 1:14 NIV

Struggling in the midst of experiences that are not fragrant, I'm thankful to know You are a sweet, exquisite bouquet, Lord. I am learning more and more to appreciate Your many facets. You are Light in the midst of my darkness, victory in the midst of my battles, and peace in the midst of my chaos. You are joy in the presence of sorrow, good in the presence of evil, and love in the presence of hate.

Yes, You are beautiful, my sweet, sweet Lord, and every trait You possess adds to the bouquet. Your fragrance soothes and settles my anxious soul. I praise Your holy name! Amen.

Everlasting Light

———— ∞ ————

"Your sun will never set again, and your moon
will wane no more; the LORD will be your everlasting
light, and your days of sorrow will end."
Isaiah 60:20 niv

The sun is so bright today, streaming through my window—it's nearly blinding. Coming on the heels of several dark and gloomy days, Lord, it lifts my spirit! It's also a great reminder that You, who lifted me from spiritual darkness, are the Everlasting Light.

Our lives are filled with so many ups and downs, lights and shadows, that stability seems nearly inconceivable, and everlasting darkness is easier to understand than everlasting light. But then You come streaming in, forcing the darkness to flee.

I praise You, God, for being the Light of the World. I worship You, the True Light that gives light to everyone. I thank You for shining brilliantly and ending the days of sorrow. Amen.

Faithful

The Maker of heaven and earth, the sea and everything in them. He remains faithful forever.
PSALM 146:6 HCSB

Faithful! Lord, You are faithful!

You called me to a task—an overwhelming task—and saw me through to the end. When I wavered, You prompted me to continue. When I bottomed out, You provided encouragement. When I thought there was absolutely no way I could do it, You made the way. It was as if I jumped into a rapid torrent—jumped in over my head—and the current of Your faithfulness kept me afloat, pushed me along, and swept me to places I couldn't get to on my own.

You are my source.

You are my strength.

You sustain.

You never quit, never give up, and never run out—for You are faithful!

I praise You, faithful Father! I exalt Your name! All glory and honor belong to You! Amen.

FORGIVER OF SINS

—⧀⧐—

I am writing to you, little children,
because your sins have been forgiven because of Jesus' name.
1 JOHN 2:12 HCSB

Gone! Wiped away! Eradicated!

As far as the sunrise is from the sunset, so far have You removed my sins from me! That's newsworthy. . . noteworthy. . .it's absolutely praiseworthy! So I praise Your name!

Without You, Jesus, I would be stuck in the past— wallowing in the muck and mire of sin. Satan would be able to accuse me constantly—and he'd be accurate. But with You, my past is just that—past—and I can move on! And Satan's accusations become lies. The truth is, I'm forgiven. I'm free. I have a future filled with hope. And it's all because of You, Jesus!

Yes, I praise the name of Jesus, the forgiver of my sins! Amen.

GOD MOST HIGH (EL ELYON)

I blessed the Most High,
and praised and honored him who lives forever.
DANIEL 4:34 ESV

Lord, You are the God Most High. There is no one like You! No one is higher. No one is mightier. No one knows more than You. You are the One who establishes and finishes. You are the One who begins and concludes. You are omnipresent, omniscient, and omnipotent—big words with big meanings, yet they still cannot contain or encompass all that You are! And because You are all these things, I can trust You. I can know that nothing will happen in my life that hasn't first been filtered through Your fingers of love. I can rest in the fact that You are able to make *all things* work together for good.

What an honor it is to call You my Lord. Why would I ever be interested in worshipping anyone or anything else? No one can measure up to You, God Most High! Amen.

GOD OF MY PRAISE

"He is your praise and He is your God, who has done for you these great and awesome works your eyes have seen."
DEUTERONOMY 10:21 HCSB

The trees lift their arms for You,
The birds take their flight for You,
The wind dances with joy for You—
How do I praise Your name?

The stars come out and shine for You,
The thunder claps from heaven for You,
The oceans rise and fall for You—
How do I promote Your fame?

God of My Praise, to You my life I raise;
Take all of me, that the world may see
The glory of You who came.
Amen.

The God of the Whole Earth

The LORD of hosts is his name; and thy Redeemer the Holy One of Israel; The God of the whole earth shall he be called.
ISAIAH 54:5 KJV

Lord of hosts!

Redeemer!

Holy One of Israel!

You are God and there is no other. You are God and there is none like You! Is there any place in heaven, on earth, or under the earth that does not belong to You?

You rule and reign from the highest heights to the deepest depths. Your kingdom extends from the tiniest microbe to the farthest galaxy—and beyond.

You laid the foundations of the earth. The heavens are the work of Your hands. You are the Lord of all—is there any other like You? I know not one!

My God—who is the God of the whole earth—I lift my voice in praise, honor, and glory to You! You are my one and only, and I worship You! Amen.

GOD OUR SAVIOR

*But after that the kindness and love of God
our Saviour toward man appeared.*
TITUS 3:4 KJV

Jesus, You are God our Savior!

God, You came because of Your kindness and love.

As Savior, You rescued us from the power of the prince of this world, transferring us from the dominion of darkness into Your glorious light.

Through Your Holy Spirit we have been regenerated . . .renewed. . .restored!

I praise You, God, for fulfilling Your promises. I lift Your name high, Jesus, for giving me peace through Your blood. I honor You, Holy Spirit, for empowering me to be Your witness.

There is none like You! Amen.

The Grain Offering

———∞———

*"When anyone brings a grain offering as an offering
to the LORD, his offering shall be of fine flour.
He shall pour oil on it and put frankincense on it."*
LEVITICUS 2:1 ESV

Holy Father, the intricate system of sacrifices and offerings
You instituted in the Old Testament seems so confusing.
They were necessary for sinful people to approach You, a
holy God. But I'm beginning to understand that You used
them not only for Your people to maintain fellowship
with You, but so all people would see Jesus—the only
offering able to give complete access to You.

Most holy Grain Offering, You offered Your perfect
life. . .for me! You poured out the oil of Your Holy Spirit,
completely surrendering Your life. . .for mine!

I worship You, Jesus, for without Your perfect offering, I would be lost. Without Your sweet sacrifice I would
have no means to approach the Father. I praise Your holy
name! Amen.

THE GREAT GOD

━━━━━ ∞ ━━━━━

For the LORD is a great God,
a great King above all gods.
PSALM 95:3 HCSB

Great are You, O God! Perfect in holiness, mighty in power—distinguished from all other gods! Your glory reaches to the heavens. All the hosts of heaven worship You!

I worship You, too, but my worship falls significantly short of Your reality. Words are inadequate. Emotions well up but can't come close to expressing Your magnitude. Even David, the psalmist, struggled to convey the immensity of Your essence. For You cannot be contained. You cannot be described. You cannot be boxed in by language.

Accept my meager efforts to worship You, O Great God. I pray You view them through the merits of Jesus, my Savior. Amen.

The Head of the Body

⫘

He is also the head of the body, the church;
He is the beginning, the firstborn from the dead,
so that He might come to have first place in everything.
COLOSSIANS 1:18 HCSB

Lord Jesus, today as in ages past, Your church is under attack. All over the globe Your body is being mistreated, persecuted, martyred. Those who oppose Your church blatantly and brutally pummel Your people, from belittling to beheading. But they don't realize their efforts only strengthen and embolden those they seek to subdue. For we know the final chapter! We know victory is Yours!

I praise You, Jesus, Head of the Body, that the gates of hell will not prevail against Your church! I praise You, Jesus, that You are supreme and preeminent in all things and over all powers, principalities, and rulers of the present darkness! For in You, all the fullness of God dwells. And through You, we are made complete. Amen.

HEALER (JEHOVAH-RAPHA)

⎯⎯⎯∞⎯⎯⎯

"I am the LORD, your healer."
EXODUS 15:26 ESV

God, I come to You today because You are the Lord who heals. You are the One who made our bodies, intricately crafting and weaving together each cell—bringing about unique, fearfully and wonderfully made individuals. You know us inside and out, even numbering the very hairs on our head! So, Lord, I know You are aware of our sicknesses and diseases. More than that, I know You have the power to heal them.

Emotionally—You set free those who are downcast, binding up the wounds of the brokenhearted (Luke 4:18; Psalm 147:3).

Physically—You take away infirmities, carrying away our diseases (Matthew 8:16–17).

Spiritually—You heal our sin-sickness—"By his wounds you have been healed" (1 Peter 2:24 NIV).

I praise You, Jehovah-Rapha, the Lord Who Heals, that I can come to You, knowing You have the power to heal completely! Amen.

I Am (Jehovah/Yahweh)

———⚬⚬⚬———

God replied to Moses, "I AM WHO I AM.
Say this to the people of Israel: I AM has sent me to you."
EXODUS 3:14 NLT

Lord, the I Am, You are the God who defies description and definition—You are perpetual. You are the God who has no boundaries—You are limitless. You are past, present, and future. Endless. Timeless. Always. Before the foundation of the world—You were. In the details of my day—You are. And in the uncertainties of the future—You will be.

I pray, O great I Am, that I may rest in Your vastness today, knowing You have my little world in Your sight and that I am secure because of Your presence. Amen.

IMMANUEL

*See, the virgin will become pregnant and give birth
to a son, and they will name Him Immanuel,
which is translated "God is with us."*
MATTHEW 1:23 HCSB

In sorrow and sadness, in joy and gladness—You are
    with me.
In trials and tests, at my worst, at my best—You are
    with me.
When life gets rough and I've had enough,
What a comfort to know that to You I can go—for
    You are with me.
O come, let us adore Him!
Amen.

Jesus

"And you shall call his name Jesus,
for he will save his people from their sins."
MATTHEW 1:21 ESV

Jesus, our preacher ended his sermon by having everyone sing "Jesus Loves Me." Initially I smiled as we sang the familiar children's song, thinking it a sweet gesture. But as we continued, the profound truths emerged from the melody, and I found myself unable to produce any sound due to the lump lodged in my throat. My eyes blurred from the tears, so I closed them and listened, silently shouting praises to Your name!

Yes, Jesus, loves me!
Yes, Jesus loves me!
Yes, Jesus loves me!
The Bible tells me so!
Amen.

Just

———— ∞ ————

"How just and upright he is!"
DEUTERONOMY 32:4 NLT

A song of Moses:

> "Listen, O heavens, and I will speak!
>   Hear, O earth, the words that I say!
> Let my teaching fall on you like rain;
>   let my speech settle like dew.
> Let my words fall like rain on tender grass,
>   like gentle showers on young plants.
> I will proclaim the name of the LORD;
>   how glorious is our God!
> He is the Rock; his deeds are perfect.
>   Everything he does is just and fair.
> He is a faithful God who does no wrong;
>   how just and upright he is!"
>   (Deuteronomy 32:1–4 NLT)

The Life

Jesus answered, "I am. . .the life."
JOHN 14:6 NIV

"For the life of the flesh is in the blood, and I have given it for you on the altar to make atonement for your souls, for it is the blood that makes atonement by the life" (Leviticus 17:11 ESV).

Lord, it sounds so gruesome and cannibalistic to thank You for washing me in Your blood. But. . .Your blood brought atonement! Your death brought life! And without the shedding of blood, there would be no forgiveness of sins!

Thank You for giving Your life, Lord Jesus, so that I might have it abundantly! May I walk throughout my day in the full knowledge that I am forgiven—I am free. You have wiped the slate clean, and I can stand before You pure, holy, blameless, without fault, and with great joy! O Jesus, the only Savior—the Way, the Truth, and the Life—I worship You this day and every day, praising You for the gift of life eternal!

Lifter of My Head

———— ✺ ————

But You, O Lord, are a shield about me,
my glory, and the One who lifts my head.
Psalm 3:3 nasb

Discouragement has set in.

Sadness encompasses me.

My body feels heavy, and movement sluggish.

But Your Word tells me that You, O Lord, are the Lifter of My Head.

You place Your hand under my chin and gently push up—causing me to shift perspective and change my view. You broaden my horizon by bringing Your truth into focus. You turn sorrow into joy, and mourning into dancing. You bring beauty from ashes.

My outlook is greatly enhanced by the uplook. I praise the One Who Lifts My Head! Amen.

LIGHT OF THE MORNING

⁓

"[The Lord] is like the morning light when the sun rises on a
cloudless morning, the glisten of rain on sprouting grass."
2 SAMUEL 23:4 HCSB

Lord, You awaken me with the promise of a fresh start. I feel the light of Your love wash over me.

As the sun rises, I recognize Your dependability, and find my comfort in You. As the breeze blows, I sense Your goodness refreshing my spirit. As I open my eyes to the beauty around me, I see Your creativity and know You are my inspiration.

Arouse me from my slumber, Lord, to notice that Your mercies are new every morning. Morning Light, awaken me to know You more! Amen.

The Living One

<hr>

*"Do not be afraid; I am the first and the last, and the living
One; and I was dead, and behold, I am alive forevermore,
and I have the keys of death and of Hades."*
REVELATION 1:17–18 NASB

My Lord Jesus, there is no other person and no other
God who can claim to be the Living One, who died
and is now alive forevermore! As the Living One, You
alone can give this full, abundant life to me because You
conquered death and Hades. As the Living One, not only
were You present at creation, but all things were created
through You—You gave them life. You have given me life
in my flesh and abundant life in my soul. And one day
very soon, You will give me new life in a new heaven and a
new earth. You are making all things new, and the dead in
Christ will rise first—all because You are the Living One
who was buried and raised on the third day according to
the scriptures!

And because death has no more victory or sting, I
will not be afraid.

Thanks be to God, who gives us the victory through
our Lord Jesus Christ—the Living One! Amen.

LORD GOD OMNIPOTENT

∞

*And I heard as it were the voice of a great multitude, and as the
voice of many waters, and as the voice of mighty thunderings,
saying, Alleluia: for the Lord God omnipotent reigneth.*
REVELATION 19:6 KJV

O Lord God Almighty, Omnipotent One—You are
matchless in glory, honor, majesty, and power. You
established the earth and all that is in it. You established
Your plan and are fulfilling every detail. In Your power,
You are coming again and will gather Your people
together—people from every nation, tribe, and tongue—
and we will celebrate the victory You gave through Jesus
Christ. For "salvation belongs to our God who sits on the
throne, and to the Lamb!" (Revelation 7:10 ESV).

Omnipotent God, the only One mighty enough to
rule and reign, there is none like You! I fall at Your feet in
worship! Amen.

LORD OF ALL

*This is the message of Good News for the people
of Israel—that there is peace with God through
Jesus Christ, who is Lord of all.*
ACTS 10:36 NLT

Of my future, present, past—You are Lord.
Of my plans, however vast—You are Lord.
Of my family, friends, foes—You are Lord.
Of my sorrows, joys, and woes—You are Lord.

No matter what comes my way,
I will walk in peace today—
    because You are Lord of All!
Amen.

Lord of Hosts (Jehovah-Sabaoth)

*Then David said to the Philistine, "You come to me with a
sword and with a spear and with a javelin, but I come
to you in the name of the LORD of hosts, the God
of the armies of Israel, whom you have defied."*
1 Samuel 17:45 esv

Lord, when David faced the giant Goliath, he did so with
great confidence. He knew who You were and what You
were capable of doing through him. The text says that
"when the Philistine arose and came and drew near to
meet David, David ran quickly toward the battle line to
meet the Philistine" (1 Samuel 17:48 esv). He ran *toward
the battle line*—not away from it! This little pip-squeak
of a guy—a total underdog—charged toward a giant the
rest of the Israelite army cowered before! Why? Because
he knew You as the Lord of Hosts. . .the God of the angel
armies. . .the God so magnificent and powerful that every
creature serves His purposes!

As I face my giants today, let me remember that I can
run toward them with David's confidence—because the
Lord of Hosts is on my side! Amen.

Maker of the Starry Host

⎯⎯⎯ ∞ ⎯⎯⎯

Look up and see: who created these? He brings out the starry host by number; He calls all of them by name. Because of His great power and strength, not one of them is missing.
ISAIAH 40:26 HCSB

Maker of the Starry Host
To You all praise is due;
You've stamped Your glory on our world
And given us our cue—
To turn our gaze toward heaven above
And focus not on me,
But recognize a bigger One
Who lives to set us free!

So I will lift my eyes toward You
And thank You that You're there;
Your awesome power and strength
So willingly You share.
Lord, let me shout my praise to You
That all the world may see—
Unmerited favor, amazing grace,
You've saved a wretch like me!

MEDIATOR

⸺ ◦◦◦◦ ⸺

There is one God and one Mediator who can reconcile
God and humanity—the man Christ Jesus.
1 TIMOTHY 2:5 NLT

Lord, I'm experiencing a new season of life as part of the "sandwich generation"—those who are raising kids and caring for aging parents simultaneously. While my family isn't super demanding, I'm still feeling the stress of being "sandwiched." At times it's overwhelming, and often I fail in my role.

But once again, I can come to You because You are able to sympathize with my weaknesses. You know exactly what it's like to feel sandwiched. The difference is, You took on that role willingly and with great success. No one else could close the gap between God and humanity. No other way could be forged to the Father except through You! You are the perfect Mediator, for You are God, yet You became man.

Completely human. Completely God. And I'm completely grateful! Amen.

MY EXCEEDING JOY

*Then I will go to the altar of God, to God my exceeding joy;
and on the harp I will praise You, O God, my God.*
PSALM 43:4 NKJV

Happiness, a high calling
Though not the highest one;
For You, O Lord, seek to draw us
To the joy of Your dear Son.

In Your presence we can know
Your joy in fullest measure;
So here I am completely bowed
And long to grasp this treasure.

Dire circumstance will not prevent
Your joy down in my heart;
Lord, You're enough—my all in all,
My Joy, my strength, my part.

My Maker

―∞∞―

Oh come, let us worship and bow down;
let us kneel before the LORD, our Maker!
PSALM 95:6 ESV

To You, Lord, we ascribe glory! To You, Father, we ascribe praise! You are the great King above all gods. You are the One who spoke the words and brought the world into existence! You formed the sun, the moon, the stars. You made colorful seas and vast landscapes. You brought forth the beauty of trees and vegetation. In Your infinite creativity, You made a crazy variety of animals. And You even created me—by knitting me together in my mother's womb. I praise You because I am fearfully and wonderfully made! You are my Maker, and I bow before You in worship. I listen for Your voice. Amen.

My Strength and My Song

❧

*"See, God has come to save me. I will trust in him
and not be afraid. The LORD GOD is my strength
and my song; he has given me victory."*
ISAIAH 12:2 NLT

You are the power—
Consuming the enemy.
My Strength and My Song.

You're the melody—
Directing each step I take.
My Strength and My Song.

I trust You, Lord God—
And I will not be afraid.
My Strength and My Song.

A Nail Fastened in a Sure Place

And I will fasten him as a nail in a sure place.
ISAIAH 22:23 KJV

Security. I've sought it from many people and places, Lord, and am finding there is no one and nothing able to offer certainty and security like You. In You there is a sense of fixedness. In You there is confidence. In You I can be completely at rest. . .knowing that whatever comes my way, You will never be taken by surprise. For You have a plan and a purpose that have been established and firmly fixed from the beginning of time. And You have the power to work that plan for Your glory.

Lord, I rest in You today. You are the Nail Fastened in a Sure Place—and I am sure of Your love for me because of the nails You bore in my place. Amen.

Perfume Poured Out

‹‹‹∞›››

Pleasing is the fragrance of your perfumes;
your name is like perfume poured out.
Song of Songs 1:3 NIV

God's virtue pours out.
My Lord's character runs deep.
It is You I love.

Rock

"There is no one besides you; there is no Rock like our God."
1 Samuel 2:2 NLT

Hannah's prayer of praise when she brought her son Samuel to Eli the priest:

"My heart rejoices in the LORD! The LORD has made me strong. Now I have an answer for my enemies; I rejoice because you have rescued me. No one is holy like the LORD! There is no one besides you; there is no Rock like our God. . . . He lifts the poor from the dust and the needy from the garbage dump. He sets them among princes, placing them in seats of honor. For all the earth is the LORD's, and he has set the world in order. He will protect his faithful ones, but the wicked will disappear in darkness. No one will succeed by strength alone." (1 Samuel 2:1–2, 8–9 NLT)

Rock of My Salvation

⎯⎯⎯ ∞ ⎯⎯⎯

"The Lord lives! Praise be to my Rock!
Exalted be my God, the Rock, my Savior!"
2 Samuel 22:47 niv

Father God, I live in awe of Your plan for me. You saved me from death through the sacrifice of Your Son, and I can stand on that promise of salvation. You are the Rock that all Your wonderful promises are built upon! There are so many shifting sands I have to deal with on a daily basis, but You remain steadfast and faithful. My heart's desire is to be dependable, to be more rock and less sand. To be like You and show others a glimpse of Your greatness. You do not change. Your value does not diminish. Your love for me doesn't change. Your grace never runs out. Your compassion abounds. Your character is true. You are God, and I exalt You. Amen.

SAVIOR

*"For unto you is born this day in the city
of David a Savior, who is Christ the Lord."*
LUKE 2:11 ESV

Born in a manger,
Born so small.
Born with a love
To cover all.
Born with a priceless
Gift to give.
Born to give me
Hope to live.

Jesus my Savior
I worship You.
There is no one to whom
More praise is due.
You gave me Your life;
Now I give You mine.
Jesus my Savior,
My heart is Thine.

SON OF MAN

―――――∞∞∞―――――

"Listen," he said, "we're going up to Jerusalem, where the Son
of Man will be betrayed to the leading priests and the teachers
of religious law. They will sentence him to die
and hand him over to the Romans."
MARK 10:33 NLT

Everlasting God,
Who willingly wore our skin,
You walked as man
As only You can,
Yet lived without one sin.

Suffering Savior,
In submitting to God's way,
You gave Your all
And took the fall,
An exorbitant price to pay.

Jesus Christ, Messiah,
Lord of lords and King of kings,
Your name I praise,
Your song I raise,
You are my everything!

Sovereign Lord (Adonai Jehovah)

But Abram said, "Sovereign Lord, what can you give me since I remain childless and the one who will inherit my estate is Eliezer of Damascus?"
Genesis 15:2 NIV

Lord, Abraham bowed his knee to You, calling You Lord and Master, even though he couldn't fathom a plan outside the tangible. He trusted You, the all-knowing Sovereign Lord, and rightly so, for You had proven Yourself faithful, powerful, and mighty.

You have proven Yourself faithful, powerful, and mighty in my life, too, Lord. I praise You that You take the unseen, unknown, and unfathomable and work them for Your glory! I bow my knee to You, O Sovereign God, submitting my will to You. For Your thoughts are higher than my thoughts, and Your ways higher than my ways. Amen.

Strong and Mighty Lord

∞

*Who is this King of glory? The L*ORD*,*
*strong and mighty, the L*ORD*, mighty in battle!*
Psalm 24:8 esv

Mighty God, the enemy is active and on the prowl. I get tired of his wily ways and so often feel like I'm at a disadvantage. But then I remember You:

You are the Lord, Strong and Mighty!

You are the Lord, mighty in battle!

You have already defeated Satan through Christ's resurrection!

Greater is He who is in me than he who is in the world!

So no matter what Satan throws at me today, I will remember that *You are greater*. He may hurl insults, lies, distraction, deception, or discouragement. He may try to undermine my peace, joy, or hope. He may cast doubt and fear my way. But God, I trust *You*. I trust Your *Word*. I trust that You are King, and no weapon formed against me shall prosper! O God, how encouraging and empowering it is to know that I am on the winning side—and You are fighting my battles. Who is this King of glory? The Lord, Strong and Mighty! Amen.

A Sure Foundation

—————∞∞∞—————

*Therefore the Lord GOD said: "Look, I have laid a stone in Zion,
a tested stone, a precious cornerstone, a sure foundation;
the one who believes will be unshakable."*
ISAIAH 28:16 HCSB

Unshakable. Not a word that often describes us, unfortunately. And Lord, You know why—we're often weak and have a tendency to waver. But Your Word says that You are solid, unwavering—a Sure Foundation! You never falter. You never fail. You are secure, a bedrock for my faith.

When nations rise and fall—You continue.

When relationships come and go—You persist.

When jobs and finances crumble—You remain.

Unshakable. A word that will forever describe You. And because You are unshakable, I can be, too.

I praise You, my Sure Foundation! Amen.

THE TRUE LIGHT

The true light, who gives light to everyone,
was coming into the world.
JOHN 1:9 HCSB

The True Light—as opposed to false lights. Lord, it seems Satan is busy sending false lights into our world—false religions, false teachers, false ideology. But false lights are just that, false. They are flawed, fictitious, concocted. They lure people in and inevitably let people down. But You, Jesus, are the True Light—pure, right, verifiable! You dispel darkness and open blinded eyes. And You are inclusive—giving light to everyone.

Lord Jesus, I praise You for shining in our dark world! Amen.

THE TRUTH

Jesus saith unto him, I am. . .the truth.
JOHN 14:6 KJV

Pilate: What is truth?
Jesus: I am the Truth.
And the truth shall set you free.

Sinner: What is truth?
Jesus: God's Word is truth.
And the truth shall set you free.

"In the beginning was the Word, and the Word was with God, and the Word was God. . . . And the Word became flesh and dwelt among us, and we have seen his glory, glory as of the only Son from the Father, full of grace and truth" (John 1:1, 14 ESV). Amen.

Unchanging

━━━━━━ ∞ ━━━━━━

"For I the Lord do not change."
Malachi 3:6 esv

Constant. Unvarying. Steady. Stable. Immutable.
It is who You are, God!
Trustworthy. Faithful. Dependable. Reliable. Unfailing.
It is why I can lean into You!
You are the same yesterday and today and forever
  (Hebrews 13:8).
Undeniable God, You are worthy of adoration!
Unchanging Savior, there is none like You!
Amen.

Warrior

The LORD is a warrior; Yahweh is His name.
EXODUS 15:3 HCSB

I'm competitive—I like to win,
Defeating foes without, within;
But my enemy doesn't seem to wane;
He launches ammo, taking aim.

Wounded from the raging battle,
I run to God who never rattles;
For on the side of Warrior God
Nothing's stacked against all odds.

Yes, He's my strength, my mighty tower,
And in my weakness He is power.
O Lord, our Warrior, Savior, Friend,
You ensured our victory! Amen!

WONDERFUL

⌒⌒⌒

For unto us a child is born, unto us a son is given. . .
and his name shall be called Wonderful.
ISAIAH 9:6 KJV

A gift given to us,
Inspiring wonder in us.
You are Wonderful.

Jesus—
May we never lose our wonder.
Amen.

The Word

*In the beginning was the Word, and the Word
was with God, and the Word was God.*
JOHN 1:1 ESV

Lord, I'm feeling pretty one-dimensional—a little shallow, even—so I'm seeking understanding.

I read that in the beginning You existed, and You are called the Word (John 1:1–2).

I read that the Word became flesh and dwelt among us (John 1:14)—and the Word was called Jesus.

I read that Jesus, who wears a robe dipped in blood, is called by a certain name—the Word of God (Revelation 19:13).

You have said that Your Word is living and active (Hebrews 4:12), that Your Word is God breathed (2 Timothy 3:16), and that Your Word gives us life (James 1:18).

Even with my one-dimensional, shallow mind, I believe You are showing me that I cannot separate You from Jesus, or Jesus from Your Word.

So I exalt the Word—Jesus Christ, the scripture, and You—above all else! Amen.

Yahweh Our Righteousness
(Jehovah-Tsidkenu)

—⟨∞⟩—

*"In His days Judah will be saved, and Israel will dwell securely.
This is what He will be named: Yahweh Our Righteousness."*
JEREMIAH 23:6 HCSB

Oh, what filthy rags I wear. I have no right to stand in
Your presence. Yet when You look at me, Lord, You don't
see the sin that condemns me to a life separated from
You. Rather, You see the glorious robe of righteousness
given to me as a gift from Your Son. The great exchange,
which took place on the cross of Calvary, delivered me
from the domain of darkness to the kingdom of light!

You are my Righteousness! Without You I am lost.

You are my restorer! Apart from You I am broken.

I praise Jesus for the right relationship I have with You!
Amen.

CONFESSION

. . .because we all miss the mark

For all have sinned and fall short of the glory of God.
ROMANS 3:23 ESV

ABBA

*And because you are sons, God has sent the Spirit of his
Son into our hearts, crying, "Abba! Father!"*
GALATIANS 4:6 ESV

Dear God, I recently read a sign that said, "I don't want to adult today. I'm done adulting." While it made me laugh, it completely struck a chord! Some days I'm tired of being the adult, and I yearn for the carefree days of childhood—days when I didn't worry about provision, protection, or security. But there's a name You wear, one that lifts the excess burdens I carry. That name is Abba—Father!

Oh, heavenly Daddy, thank You for promising that You'll take care of me. Forgive me for not trusting You with those details. Worrying won't help anything—in fact, it's a sin obstructing me from worshipping You! So today, let me crawl up in Your lap, feel the warmth of Your embrace, and relinquish my false sense of control. I rest in You, Abba. I trust You, Daddy. I worship You, Father. Amen.

Advocate

⸻

*My little children, I am writing these things to you so
that you may not sin. But if anyone does sin, we have an
advocate with the Father, Jesus Christ the righteous.*
1 John 2:1 esv

I've fallen, Lord. I've stumbled and sinned and marred
Your reputation. Nothing in me is worthy of You. . .of
Your love. Yet You've seen fit to give me an Advocate in
Jesus Christ. I'm not quite sure how He accomplishes it,
but somehow You hear Him and trust Him and see His
righteousness and not my filthy rags. It's upside down,
Lord. I don't deserve this gift of Jesus Christ. Maybe
that's why Your grace is called amazing. So I thank You.
Amen.

ALL AND IN ALL

In this new life, it doesn't matter if you are a Jew or a Gentile, circumcised or uncircumcised, barbaric, uncivilized, slave, or free. Christ is all that matters, and he lives in all of us.
COLOSSIANS 3:11 NLT

Heavenly Father, it's pretty amazing to think that from one man, You made every nation of humankind. If records allowed, we could all trace our family tree back to the exact same root! The diversity of tribes, tongues, nations, and peoples is part of Your great creation. But like most things, we've taken Your beautiful template and twisted it until it is no longer recognizable. Hatred, jealousy, pride, disdain—tools we've used to dismantle Your design. Even in the church, Lord, we've drawn random lines of distinction, separating those who are "in" and those who are "out."

And I'm part of the problem. Forgive me, Father, for shunning and shaming.

As You have opened the doors of salvation through Jesus Christ to everyone, let me be Your greeter—and freely offer the acceptance You have shown me! For Christ is all that matters. He is our All in All! Amen.

All-Sufficient One (El Shaddai)

—∞∞∞—

But he said to me, "My grace is sufficient for you."
2 CORINTHIANS 12:9 NIV

Surrendered. Lord, this is my goal.

Fully yielding my life to You seems like it should be an easy objective, as You are a good and merciful God. You gave the best You have to offer—Your only Son—to cover my sins. You provide for every single need, giving abundantly more than I could ever ask or think. You supply guidance, counsel, and wisdom. You protect. You love me with an everlasting love—something You've proven over and over again. You are faithful. In essence, You are all I need—my All-Sufficient One!

So why do I struggle to completely relinquish everything to You? How can I sing "I Surrender All" when I'm withholding pieces of my heart and clinging to a self-appointed pseudosupremacy? Forgive me, Lord! This battle for control is real. It's no wonder You tell us to take up our cross *daily*, for it's a *daily* death of self, a *daily* surrender of control, a *daily* renewal of commitment.

So today, I surrender yet again.

ARCHITECT AND BUILDER

*For he was looking forward to the city that has foundations,
whose architect and builder is God.*
HEBREWS 11:10 HCSB

God, You are a master designer. That truth is confirmed
when I look at the world around me—I see design;
therefore, there *is* a designer! And You, the Architect and
Builder of that design, have an all-encompassing vantage
point that allows You to orchestrate all things for our
good and Your glory.

But sometimes, God, I forget that truth. Sometimes
I question the master blueprint. Sometimes "self" takes
over and I only consider *my* situation, *my* feelings, and *my*
ease. Lord, I'm sorry.

Father, as Abraham trusted You, may I trust You. He
saw the promises from afar and understood the bigger,
better design. Please continue to work on me, shifting
my attention from temporal to eternal and my focus from
self to Savior.

You are the Master Architect—build in me what You
will. Amen.

BANNER FOR THE PEOPLES

In that day the Root of Jesse will stand as a banner
for the peoples; the nations will rally to him,
and his resting place will be glorious.
ISAIAH 11:10 NIV

Lord Jesus, I read Your Word and see that when You are lifted up, people seek after You. And after reading this, I'm convicted that I've not done the best job of lifting You up. I've misrepresented You—failing to reveal Your beauty and holiness, withholding love and mercy from those who desperately need You.

I ask You to forgive me, Lord. I ask You to forgive all of us who are Your representatives. Save us from misrepresentation. I ask that Jesus, the Banner, be reflected through lives of grace and truth—and that it begin in me.

May I lift You high, Jesus, Banner for the Peoples, that the world may rally to You and be saved. Amen.

The Branch

—∞∞∞—

*"Listen, Joshua the high priest, you and your colleagues
sitting before you; indeed, these men are a sign that
I am about to bring My servant, the Branch."*
ZECHARIAH 3:8 HCSB

Humble beginnings. It's how You work. And in a world
that magnifies self, it totally defies expectations. Though
You are the almighty God, You submitted Yourself to
the Father. Though You are independently capable, You
attached Yourself to Him. Even Your name, the Branch,
suggests controlled strength—a beautiful meekness.

You've set an example for me to follow, Jesus—
showing what it looks like to abide in the Vine. As You
were dependent on the Father, I pray I will be dependent
on You. I must confess the abiding doesn't happen
consistently, though. I detach on occasion—I go rogue.
But because of Your indwelling Spirit, I recognize the
fruitlessness of those endeavors and remember that apart
from You, I can do nothing (John 15:5).

Lord, I want to abide in You. Lord, I want to be like
You. Lord, let me begin like You—with humility. Amen.

Chiefest among Ten Thousand

⸺⊗⊗⊗⸺

My beloved is white and ruddy,
the chiefest among ten thousand.
Song of Solomon 5:10 KJV

Ten thousand. That's about the number of things on my to-do list today—and every day! But can I say, that of all those on my list, You are the highest priority? Theoretically? Yes. Practically? If I'm being honest. . .the answer would have to be no.

Lord, I let so many other people and things crowd You out. It's confession time: busyness has become my god. I hold it up and esteem it for everyone to see. But even more pathetic—I expect everyone to admire me for doing so! How warped is that, God?

Oh, forgive me for having other gods before You! Forgive me for not giving You the honor, praise, and position You are due. For You are the God of gods, King of kings, Lord of lords! You are the Chiefest among Ten Thousand!

Lord, the to-do list will not go away, and busyness will still be a part of my day. But I pray that You will take first place in the minutes and hours before me. And if my priorities get out of whack, may Your Holy Spirit prompt me to reorganize! You are my highest priority. I love You. Amen.

Christ Jesus

＊＊＊

*This is a trustworthy saying, and everyone should accept it:
"Christ Jesus came into the world to save sinners"—
and I am the worst of them all.*
1 Timothy 1:15 nlt

"I am the worst of them all."

The apostle Paul said this about himself, Lord, and it hardly seems accurate! He's the writer of most of our doctrine. He's probably in the all-time top ten of those who led people to Christ. But he's also the same one who wrote, "I do not do what I want, but I do the very thing I hate" (Romans 7:15 esv), and "All have sinned and fall short of the glory of God" (Romans 3:23 esv). Obviously, sin is a problem for all of us, and if we're honest, we could all write the same words as Paul, "I am the worst." The real issue, though, is that this sin broke our relationship with You, God.

But praise be to Christ Jesus who came into this world to save sinners and restore that relationship! Jesus, I bow in Your presence and pour out my soul in gratitude to You. Thank You for saving me, the worst sinner of all. Amen.

The Chosen of God

—— ∞∞∞ ——

And the people stood beholding. And the rulers also
with them derided him, saying, He saved others;
let him save himself, if he be Christ, the chosen of God.
LUKE 23:35 KJV

Jesus, You are the Chosen of God. God chose *You.* He chose
You because You were the only One who could meet His
requirements—perfect, blameless, sinless. You were the only
One capable of laying down Your life and raising it up again.
You were the only One who loved the world so completely
that You gave up everything—*everything*—to give the
hopeless a hope that would never disappoint.

If God, the Creator and Maker of the universe—the
One with ultimate wisdom and knowledge—chose You,
why would I ever consider choosing anyone or anything
else above You? Yet I do. At times I have chosen my family over You. . .my comfort over You. . .my career, dreams,
and desires over You. Lord, forgive me! Today, I choose
You—and if other people or things try to usurp Your
rightful position, let me remember Your name, the Chosen of God! Amen.

COMMANDER

❦

*"Behold, I have made him a witness to the peoples,
a leader and commander for the peoples."*
ISAIAH 55:4 NASB

Lord, we are living in a time when everyone is doing what is right in their own eyes. Moral relativism permeates every facet of society—just as in the era of the biblical judges. We're watching a whole generation grow up who don't know You or what You have done. We're losing our ability to recognize Your right to command.

Bring us back to You! You are a leader and Commander deserving of respect and obedience. You are the all-powerful, all-knowing, almighty God who has given Your Son so that we might have life—and we are squandering that gift. Lord, I pray we humble ourselves and seek Your face! May it begin with me. Amen.

CREATOR OF ALL THINGS

——∞∞∞——

For by him were all things created.
COLOSSIANS 1:16 KJV

Lord, You are the Creator of the heavens and the earth—all things visible and invisible. The magnitude of this truth escapes me, but when I finally take a moment to ponder Your vastness and infinite power, I'm reminded of my smallness.

> When I look at your heavens, the work of your fingers, the moon and the stars, which you have set in place, what is man that you are mindful of him, and the son of man that you care for him? (Psalm 8:3–4 ESV)

I ask with the psalmist, Father—why do You pay any attention to me? I build myself up by tearing others down. I seek my own glory, usurping what rightfully belongs to You. I focus on my kingdom, neglecting Yours. Even in prayer, the pronoun of choice centers on me.

Pride.

Vanity.

Selfish ambition.

O Father, forgive me for not reflecting the glory *You* deserve!

O Lord, how majestic *You* are in all the earth! Amen.

EXCELLENT

Let them praise the name of the LORD: for his name alone is excellent; his glory is above the earth and heaven.
PSALM 148:13 KJV

Lord, I hear so many take Your name in vain, using Your name in demeaning and vulgar ways. It infuriates me! But then I think about how I don't give You the honor You're due—and I realize I'm throwing stones from my own glass house. For You are high and lofty. You are mighty and strong. You are the Creator—the One who made our mouths so we can speak—and yet we, the created, use that same mouth to deride You and Your creation.

Forgive us, Father. We've lost sight of our position. We've neglected to recognize the proper place and praise You command. For Your name is Excellent, and You are exalted in majesty above all the earth and heaven.

Lord, I desire to honor You with my lips.

Lord, I long to esteem You with my thoughts.

Lord, I pray that the words of my mouth and the meditations of my heart be acceptable in Your sight. Amen.

FAITHFUL AND TRUE

⸺ ∘∾∘ ⸺

Then I saw heaven opened, and there was a white horse.
Its rider is called Faithful and True.
REVELATION 19:11 HCSB

Lord, when I look back over the days, years, and decades of my life, a truth emerges—You have not changed. I've been all over the map—physically, emotionally, spiritually—but You have remained constant. When I've messed up, You've been there to forgive me. When I've run to You, Your arms have been opened wide. When I've called to You, You've answered.

Lord, as I've gone about the process of living, I'm ashamed to think how often I've taken You for granted—how often I've forgotten Your nature. Forgive me. The evidence of Your character abounds, and I'm blind and forgetful.

As I move forward, Lord, I ask that the scales fall from my eyes and my memory be sharpened. Let my new vision and vibrant recollection propel me to confidently walk in Your plan—for You are the Faithful and True God. Amen.

FORTRESS

*The LORD is my rock, and my fortress, and my deliverer; my
God, my strength, in whom I will trust; my buckler, and the
horn of my salvation, and my high tower.*
PSALM 18:2 KJV

Father, I confess I'm scared. Terror is running rampant in
our world and our nation. A vernacular of vitriol spews
from the airwaves and around the watercoolers. Tensions
are high and people are snapping. Lives are cut short and
fear looms large.

God, cover me. Be my refuge and Fortress. Lord, de-
liver me by placing Your angel around me, for Your Word
says, "The angel of the LORD encamps around those who
fear him, and he delivers them" (Psalm 34:7 NIV).

That's the answer, isn't it, Lord? As I have prayed
Your Word, You have shown me the problem: my fear has
been misplaced. As I have sought You, You have revealed
the solution: shift the fear—from the terror of man to the
reverence of You.

Thank You for using Your Word to fortify my
defenses. Thank You for being my Fortress! Amen.

A Glorious Throne
to His Father's House

 ∞

He shall be for a glorious throne to his father's house.
Isaiah 22:23 kjv

Lord, Your Word says that we can come boldly to the throne of grace so that we may obtain mercy and find grace in our time of need. Well, I'm needy. I'm struggling in my ability to extend grace. There are so many in our world who are against You—against Your people. They ridicule Your standards and scoff at Your sovereignty. It angers me, Lord! Rather than praying for my enemies, I find myself wanting to see them shut down and cut off.

So, Jesus, I come before Your throne—the place where You grant unmerited favor to me—one who was formerly far off; an alien; a child of wrath; dead in my trespasses and sins. I ask that You empower me, Your new creation, to be a conduit of that same grace. I pray that Your mercy flow out to the unlikely and undeserving—for it is by grace I have been saved. Amen.

GOD (ELOHIM)

Create in me a clean heart, O God,
and renew a right spirit within me.
PSALM 51:10 ESV

A psalm of David, regarding the time Nathan the prophet came to him after David had committed adultery with Bathsheba:

Have mercy on me, O God,
because of your unfailing love.
Because of your great compassion,
blot out the stain of my sins.
Wash me clean from my guilt.
Purify me from my sin.
For I recognize my rebellion;
it haunts me day and night.
Against you, and you alone, have I sinned;
I have done what is evil in your sight.
You will be proved right in what you say,
and your judgment against me is just.
(Psalm 51:1–4 NLT)

GUIDE

*You will lead the people You have redeemed with Your
faithful love; You will guide them to Your
holy dwelling with Your strength.*
EXODUS 15:13 HCSB

I will wait upon the Lord
and He will be my Guide.
I will trust the Lord
and He will be my strength.
In my youth I waited expectantly.
In my "wisdom" I rush and pass Him by.
As a youth, my life was in His hands.
As time goes on, I forget—
And trust in my own failing hands.
I will wait upon the Lord
and He will be my Guide.
I will trust in the Lord
and He will be my strength.

HEALER (JEHOVAH-RAPHA)

Heal me, O LORD, and I will be healed;
save me and I will be saved, for You are my praise.
JEREMIAH 17:14 NASB

Lord, what a comfort to know that You are my balm. . .
my Healer! I'm so grateful that You saw fit to heal me
of my sin-sickness on an eternal level. Even though that
is more than I deserve, You continue to give—for on a
temporal level, You heal and bring relief as well. Lord, my
sin caused the brokenness in our relationship. Help me
not to forget that sin can cause other problems, too—so
the sooner I run to You, the sooner You can expose the
disease and heal.

And, Lord, as I experience Your restoration in my
life—emotionally, physically, and spiritually—may I be
quick in declaring Your name and long in remembering
Your goodness. For by Your wounds I am healed. Amen.

Holy One of Israel
(Qedosh Yisrael)

⚬⚬⚬

*This is what the LORD says—the Redeemer and Holy One
of Israel—to him who was despised and abhorred by the
nation, to the servant rulers: "Kings will see you and stand
up, princes will see and bow down, because of the LORD,
who is faithful, the Holy One of Israel, who has chosen you."*
ISAIAH 49:7 NIV

Isaiah saw You, Lord, in all Your glory. He heard the
seraphim declare, "Holy, holy, holy is the LORD of hosts"
(Isaiah 6:3 HCSB). He hadn't fully recognized Your holiness
until that point, but when he did, his unworthiness
became glaringly apparent.

I've not been cognizant of Your holiness, Lord. Your
glory, purity, power, mystery, and otherness are difficult
to comprehend. But I know in my everyday living I've
made You common—the One who is uncommon. In
my thoughts and words I've profaned Your name—the
One whose name will cause every knee to bow and every
tongue to confess that You are indeed Lord!

Purify me, Holy One of Israel. Cleanse me. Make me
holy because You are the only One capable. Amen.

Husband

*"For your Maker is your husband—
the LORD Almighty is his name."*
ISAIAH 54:5 NIV

Jesus, lover of our souls, You are our Husband and the church is Your bride. You desire for us to be faithful to You—pure, holy, and blameless—adorned in white. But we have strayed and have stained our robes of righteousness. We've been lured by the longing to be popular. Our lust for cultural acceptance denies Your power and diminishes Your glory. We've watered down truth to tickle the ears of the populace, and offered milk rather than meat, malnourishing Your priesthood.

Forgive us, dear Lord. Cleanse us of our sins. Wash us, and we will be whiter than snow! And when we have turned our hearts back to You, I pray You would embolden us to stand on Your Word, empower us to walk in Your way, and encourage us to worship in grace and in truth. In the name of Jesus, the Lord Almighty, I pray. Amen.

KING

<hr>

Let the king be enthralled by your beauty;
honor him, for he is your lord.
PSALM 45:11 NIV

Wow! Jealousy has reared its ugly head! My words were pure vitriol, and I'm ashamed. God, why can't I celebrate when good things happen to someone? Why can't words of encouragement be my norm? Am I so insecure that in order to build myself up, I must tear someone else down?

Forgive me, Lord! I have sinned.

Yet because of Your great love, and the work of Christ on the cross, I can know that I am forgiven!

And You take it one step further by building me up with words of encouragement. You, my King, are enthralled with my beauty? When You look at me, You don't see the ugly sin—You see the beauty of Christ!

So may I honor You, Lord, by honoring others. Let me celebrate with them. Let me speak words of grace to a world desperate for approval. Amen.

The King in His Beauty

Your eyes will see the King in His beauty;
you will see a vast land.
Isaiah 33:17 HCSB

Jesus, You said, "Blessed are the pure in heart, for they will see God" (Matthew 5:8 NIV). Sometimes I look for You, but I don't see You. Is it because of sin? Am I harboring bitterness? Unforgiveness? Pride? Selfishness? Greed? Idolatry? Immorality? So often I look at the "other guy" and find all manner of evil in him, but I quickly overlook or dismiss areas in my own life where I miss the mark. It seems I've been splinter searching when logs are lodged in my own life.

Forgive me, Lord. I long to see You. Cleanse me. Purify me. You promise that when I confess my sins, You are faithful and just and will forgive me of all unrighteousness (1 John 1:9)! Thank You for Your faithfulness, even when I am unfaithful. Thank You for allowing me to gaze on Your beauty again, my King! Amen.

KING OF KINGS

∞

*And it shall come to pass, that every one that is left of all
the nations which came against Jerusalem shall even go
up from year to year to worship the King, the LORD of
hosts, and to keep the feast of tabernacles.*
ZECHARIAH 14:16 KJV

Lord, if I'm in the presence of big-name preachers, I want
to hang out with them—sit at their feet and soak up their
wisdom. I want them to know my name—to know me.

But I've recognized I've grossly misplaced my adoration! How odd that my desire is to be noticed by flawed
men. How crazy that I pay homage and lofty compli-
ments to mere men and neglect to lift You high, the King
of kings and Lord of lords. How wrong that I seek wisdom and acknowledgment from them instead of You.

Forgive me, O King. You are the One of whom I
should make much, because there is none like You. Amen.

The Living Bread

∞

"I am the living bread that came down from heaven."
JOHN 6:51 HCSB

Lord, I've been eating a lot of unhealthy foods lately—with an attitude that I have a right to eat what I want, when I want. But my rights seem to be backfiring! I'm lethargic, run down, and overweight. My demeanor has changed, too, and affected my family, friends, and ministry. It's a snowball effect!

Lord, help! Help me understand my body is Your temple and should be treated as such. I surrender my rights to You. I surrender my ways to You. I ask You to shift my hunger and thirst from the physical to the spiritual. Let me taste and see that You are good. . .that Your words are sweeter than honey. . .that You, the Living Bread, can satisfy and nourish my soul unlike anything else. I long to be filled with You, Lord Jesus. Amen.

THE LORD GOD
(ADONAI ELOHIM)

❦

So I turned my attention to the Lord God to seek Him
by prayer and petitions, with fasting, sackcloth, and ashes.
DANIEL 9:3 HCSB

Daniel's prayer of confession for the people of Israel:

"Ah, Lord—the great and awe-inspiring God who keeps His gracious covenant with those who love Him and keep his commands—we have sinned, done wrong, acted wickedly, rebelled, and turned away from Your commands and ordinances. We have not listened to Your servants the prophets, who spoke in your name to our kings, leaders, fathers, and all the people of the land.

Lord, righteousness belongs to You, but this day public shame belongs to us. . . . LORD, public shame belongs to us. . .because we have sinned against You. Compassion and forgiveness belong to the Lord our God, though we have rebelled against Him and have not obeyed the voice of the LORD our God by following His instructions that He set before us through His servants the prophets." (Daniel 9:4–10 HCSB)

The Lord Is There
(Jehovah-Shammah)

———— ∞ ————

"And the name of the city from that time
on shall be, The LORD Is There."
EZEKIEL 48:35 ESV

The Lord Is There. Thank You for showing me this name today, Father, for it's a name that reminds me of Your presence. So often I try to go it alone...fly solo. Sometimes I think I might be bothering You with my petty issues, so I don't seek counsel from You regarding my plans. Other times I think I'm pretty smart—so I don't consult You as I carry out my plans. Then there are occasions I just want to do what I want to do—so I don't even contemplate Your involvement.

That's wrong—on every level. And I'm sure it's hurtful, too.

Yet You are there. You've never left. I'm the one who shunned Your presence. In fact, You promised You would never leave or forsake me. You're always there waiting for me.

Lord—God Who Is There—I don't want to make You wait for me again. I don't want to fly solo! I need You—Your guidance, Your counsel, Your presence. Forgive me for neglecting You. Amen.

MANNA

Now the house of Israel called its name manna.
EXODUS 16:31 ESV

Lord, I know the story—how every day, for forty years, while they wandered around the wilderness, the Israelites went out to gather manna. It was Your provision. It was how You fed Your people and kept them alive. But they considered only themselves and hoarded it—causing it to stink and rot. They got tired of it and grumbled and complained against You—completely missing the wonder of Your sustaining miracle.

Even today, You've not ceased to sustain Your people, Lord. You are our Manna. We can feast on You—the Word of God. But I confess, sometimes I think only of myself and don't share You with others. Sometimes I take for granted what You've given, and my attitude toward You stinks. Sometimes I come to Your Word and miss the miracle of Your provision. I lose the wonder of You. Jesus, my daily Manna, let me savor Your words, for they sustain. . .they are life. Let me taste and see again, that You are good. Amen.

Merciful

"Be merciful, just as your Father also is merciful."
LUKE 6:36 HCSB

A double standard—
Judging, withholding mercy,
Yet needing the same.

A new commandment—
Because I've been forgiven,
Love one another.

MIGHTY GOD

⚬⚬⚬

For a child is born to us, a son is given to us.
The government will rest on his shoulders.
And he will be called. . .Mighty God.
ISAIAH 9:6 NLT

Lord, why do I doubt Your power? Why do I question Your might? Why do I fear and fret when a foe threatens? You are the *Mighty God*! You have made the heavens and the earth and nothing is too difficult for You. You have overcome enemies with Your mighty right arm. You have defeated Satan through Your death, burial, and resurrection! And You have promised that I am more than a conqueror because of Your great love.

Because of You, I can be sure that nothing will ever separate us from Your love. Death can't, and life can't. The angels can't, and the demons can't. Our fears for today, our worries about tomorrow, and even the powers of hell can't keep Your love away. Whether we are high above the sky or in the deepest ocean, "nothing in all creation will ever be able to separate us" from the love of our Mighty God (Romans 8:38–39 NLT). Amen.

Morning Star

"And I will give him the morning star."
REVELATION 2:28 NKJV

Lord, the world is dark, for it lies in the lap of the devil. And I confess—I've gotten comfortable in the dim lighting. My eyes have acclimated. I've grown accustomed to certain "acceptable" sins.

But You, Lord, have given us the Morning Star—the light of Christ—to shine into our world and expose evil for what it is. You are the ray of light dispelling darkness. You are a radiant beam drawing us to Yourself.

Morning Star, shine in our world! Shine in my life! Forgive me for settling in and getting comfortable with sin. Like a laser, may Your light cut out anything in my life that is contrary to Your will. Keep my eyes fixed on You. Keep me ready for Your return. Amen.

My Adequacy

⬥⬥⬥

Not that we are adequate in ourselves to consider anything as coming from ourselves, but our adequacy is from God.
2 CORINTHIANS 3:5 NASB

Lord, I'm at the end of my abilities, but I keep trying to muster more from within. As if.

As if I have more to give.

As if I have something to say.

As if I have an untapped resource.

But then You remind me that I do—and it has nothing to do with me, but everything to do with *You*! You are my resource! You are my wellspring of life! You are my sufficiency, competency, and *Adequacy*! All I need I have in You, Lord.

Forgive me for trying to work on my own. It must hurt You so much to watch me attempt to muscle my way through each day without connecting to You, the source of true strength. I confess this as sin and ask Your forgiveness. I pray You would empower me to break this habit and to replace it by practicing Your presence each day. Amen.

My Helper

Therefore, we may boldly say: The Lord is my helper;
I will not be afraid. What can man do to me?
HEBREWS 13:6 HCSB

Lord, fear is my enemy. It lurks and lunges. It creeps and controls. And I'm over it! I'm done with its teasing and torment. I've allowed fear in my life—revealing my lack of trust in You. Father, forgive me. I know You are greater than fear! Your Word states that I can *boldly* say, "You are my Helper!" and fear will no longer master me.

Therefore. . .because You are my Helper,

I do not have to fear man.

I do not have to fear sickness.

I do not have to fear failure.

I do not have to fear the future.

Lord, my Helper, I run to You and find refuge and peace in who You are! I rest in You, knowing You will never leave or forsake me. What an amazing promise! What an amazing God! Amen.

My Husband

———◇◇◇———

*"In that day," declares the LORD, "you will call me 'my husband';
you will no longer call me 'my master.'"*
HOSEA 2:16 NIV

Lord, You are the lover of my soul, yet I don't treat You
that way. Sometimes I get bogged down in a checklist
of behaviors, good deeds, and thou-shalt-nots. When I
do this, I'm missing out on the sweet relationship You
desire—a relationship built on love and trust and seeking
the other's best interest.

Forgive me for treating You as a taskmaster. Revive
my love for You. For I am Your church—Your bride. And
You are my Husband. Amen.

My Portion

Whom have I in heaven but you? And there is nothing on earth that I desire besides you. My flesh and my heart may fail, but God is the strength of my heart and my portion forever.
PSALM 73:25–26 ESV

Father, after a fantastic meal I'm stuffed! But incredibly, I know I'll want to eat again in a few hours. I've learned that my meals cannot satisfy.

If I buy a new car—the nicest car I've ever had—and think I'll never want another, it's only a matter of time before it starts to show wear and I find myself looking at other, newer vehicles. Obviously, my car cannot satisfy.

I could remodel my kitchen with freshly painted cabinets, trendy countertops, and pristine appliances. But I imagine in a few years, I'll want to upgrade and update as these, too, will never satisfy.

But You, Lord, are One who *does* satisfy. You fulfill, You complete, You remain.

Lord, I recognize discontentment has settled into my heart—and it's ugly. So I confess it today and claim You as my Portion! Lord, You fill all and are in all. Be my all today. Amen.

My Rock

For You are my rock and my fortress;
You lead and guide me because of Your name.
PSALM 31:3 HCSB

Father, I heard about a sinkhole in a parking lot. I was shocked when I saw the size! Two cars could have easily been swallowed up, had they been there when the earth gave way.

Sometimes I feel like I'm close to being swallowed up, too—by deadlines, expectations, schedules, and responsibilities. So I shore up my foundation by trying harder and doing more, only to find the earth starts giving way again.

Lord, I realize I'm not so great at "shoring up" on my own. My support systems give way when they aren't built on You. Forgive me for trying to manage life by myself—in my own strength. Today, I establish myself on You, my Rock. Lead me and guide me because of Your name. Amen.

The Only God

⚒

To the only God our Savior. . .
JUDE 1:25 NASB

Heavenly Father, we're living in politically correct times. You can't call things what they really are because it's considered offensive. Instead, everyone goes about their business denying truth—celebrating the emperor's "clothes" rather than acknowledging he's naked! The same holds true for our worship. We praise and lift on high our sports teams, busy schedules, money, careers, cars, houses, education, children, and even ministries. We give these things top priority—calling them blessings when the reality is, they have become our gods, usurping Your rightful place in our lives.

Lord, You are the only authentic God. You are the only One worthy of praise. Forgive us for replacing You with illegitimate substitutes. Draw our hearts back to You so that we might realign our priorities to the Only God! Amen.

RANSOM

⚯

*"For even the Son of Man came not to be served but to serve,
and to give his life as a ransom for many."*
MARK 10:45 ESV

Ransom (*ran*-suhm)—to redeem from captivity or bondage by paying a demanded price.

My sin brought me here—
Shackled. Imprisoned. Fettered.
Is there any hope?

Holiness given—
Inequitable exchange!
Hope's name is Jesus.

Restorer

He restores my soul;
He leads me in the paths of righteousness
for His name's sake.
PSALM 23:3 NKJV

O Father, I am so grateful that You are the Restorer! Your name is at stake, so when I do anything that compromises Your reputation, make me aware of my sin. Convict me through Your Spirit. Stop my straying and guide me back to Your right path.

Prompt me.

Prod me.

Pull me.

Whatever it takes, Lord, for my heart's desire is to exalt Your name! Amen.

RIGHTEOUS JUDGE

⎯⎯⎯∞⎯⎯⎯

But the LORD sits enthroned forever; he has established
his throne for justice, and he judges the world with
righteousness; he judges the peoples with uprightness.
PSALM 9:7–8 ESV

Lord, so many injustices happen every day, and it seems the wicked continue to get away with murder—literally! People who flaunt evil, taking advantage of the "little guys," pile up riches and grow in popularity, while those who follow the rules get trampled underfoot. Sometimes I find myself angry and envious. But that's when I know it's time to look through a wide-angle lens. It's time to remember who You are!

Lord, You are the Righteous Judge, faithful and loving. "Righteousness and justice are the foundation of your throne; steadfast love and faithfulness go before you" (Psalm 89:14 ESV). You've got this! I don't have to worry about corrupt courts having their way or wrongs never being righted. For Your court is just, and Your ways are right.

Thank You for allowing me into Your presence to adjust my perspective and settle my concerns. Forgive me for being irritated, revealing my lack of trust in You. You are trustworthy. You are bigger than my worries. You sit enthroned forever. You are God! Amen.

Savior of the World

∞

We have seen and testify that the Father
has sent the Son to be the Savior of the world.
1 John 4:14 nasb

Savior of the World,
>   You paid the price for my sin.
>   It should have been me.

SERVANT

—∞—

*Have this mind among yourselves, which is yours in Christ
Jesus. . .[who] emptied himself, by taking the form of a servant.*
PHILIPPIANS 2:5, 7 ESV

Jesus, You willingly left the glory of heaven and submitted
to the will of the Father—even to the point of death. In so
doing, You gave us the ultimate example of what it looks
like to serve, to submit, to humble oneself. You've called
me to have that same attitude by considering others more
highly than myself. But today, I failed You. I wanted my
side heard. I wanted my way done. And the entire time,
I *knew* I was not being obedient to You. I *knew* I wasn't
serving my friend. And even when Your Spirit prompted
me to apologize, I didn't.

Lord, that was so wrong—it wasn't what You would
have done. So right now I want to apologize to You. I'm
sorry to disappoint You over and over again. I'm sorry I
go against Your will and Your commands. My prideful
attitude does not reflect Christ in me. Please forgive me.

Lord, I know what I need to do next—have a
much-needed conversation with the one I've hurt. I pray
Your name will be honored through my words and actions. I pray that You will become more as I become less.
Amen.

Shepherd (Jehovah-Raah)

————∞————

"My sheep hear my voice,
and I know them, and they follow me."
John 10:27 esv

Dear Father, my mind is going a million miles an hour! I'm preoccupied with planning, worrying about what-ifs, and majoring in the minors. The cacophony of chaos deafens, preventing me from hearing Your voice.

I'm ashamed that I've muted Your voice with what amounts to white noise, Lord. Forgive me for paying homage to the idol of worry. Still my mind, Jesus. Calm my spirit, dear Shepherd. Open my ears to hear what You have to say. It is Your voice I long to listen to, Your words I yearn to perceive.

You are my Shepherd. I am Your sheep. Lord, I will follow You. Amen.

Showers That Water the Earth

May he be like rain that falls on the mown grass,
like showers that water the earth!
PSALM 72:6 ESV

Lord, I've seen unwatered plants. They look pitiful—so limp and lifeless. Long neglected, they've gone dry. As I reflect on that image, it seems You've given me a glimpse of my own spiritual state. I confess that I've let my relationship with You desiccate. I've not sought nourishment from Your Word. I've neglected fellowship with Your people. I've been silent in prayer. Those combined make for a depleted soul—a limp and lifeless soul.

Father, forgive me for paying attention to everything and everyone else. Help me seek You again—seek You first. Saturate the soil of my life, for You, O Lord, are like Showers That Water the Earth! Amen.

SIN PURGER

—————〰————

When He had by Himself purged our sins,
[Jesus] sat down at the right hand of the Majesty on high.
HEBREWS 1:3 NKJV

Lord, I take sin too lightly. It is so common and so accepted that sometimes I don't even think of it as being problematic. Truth is, one sin makes a sinner and shuts the door to heaven. And I met that requirement years ago. But You, Jesus, came as the Sin Purger, cleansing humankind from sin and opening that door for anyone who believes in You as Christ and bows to You as Lord!

I believe. . .and I bow.

Jesus, I'm sorry I go about my day—involved in my routine—not taking time to tell others of this cleansing! You opened the door to heaven for me. I pray I will look for opportunities to share this life-altering story today. I ask for tender hearts for those who hear it—that they, too, might know the great cleansing only the Sin Purger can give. Amen.

TEACHER

*"But do not be called Rabbi; for One is your Teacher,
and you are all brothers."*
MATTHEW 23:8 NASB

Jesus, so many voices and opinions are floating around—
everyone acting as if they are the ultimate authority. And
because there are so many voices, sometimes Yours gets
drowned out. I listen to the loud ones, the confident
ones. . .which usually turn out to be the wrong ones. I
get caught up in the trends, and I neglect the truth. If I'm
honest, sometimes I just want to go the easy route, the
wide road—quite a detour from the straight and narrow.

Forgive me for not listening to You. Forgive me for
my laziness. Forgive me for being idle. The hard truth is
that ease has become my idol. I pray I set my heart and
mind to diligently seek You, Jesus. Let me put forth effort and listen for Your voice. Let me sit at Your feet and
learn from You, for You are my Teacher. Your Holy Spirit
guides and leads into all truth. Amen.

TENDER GRASS

And he shall be. . .as the tender grass springing out
of the earth by clear shining after rain.
2 SAMUEL 23:4 KJV

Lord, as the tender grass is the perfect nourishment for sheep, so You are the perfect sustenance for me. Lord, I confess I don't feed on You, the Living Word, like I need to. I neglect Your Word too often. . .and even when I read it, I don't properly digest it or apply it to my life.

I pray today that will change. I don't want to be a spiritual infant, living on milk, being unskilled in the word of righteousness. It's time to move on to solid food, fully feasting on the meat of Your Word, being trained by constant practice to discern good from evil (Hebrews 5:12–14).

Lord, my Tender Grass, open my eyes to see the wonderful things in Your Word (Psalm 119:18)! Amen.

A Witness to the People

⌘

*"Behold, I have made him a witness to the peoples,
a leader and commander for the peoples."*
Isaiah 55:4 NASB

Father God, everything about Jesus pointed to You. He was Your Witness. His words, actions, temperament—all explained You to the world. So in tune was He with You that He said, "Anyone who has seen me has seen the Father" (John 14:9 NIV). So united was He with You that He said, "I and the Father are one" (John 10:30 NIV).

Lord, You have called me to be like Jesus.

You have commanded me to abide in You.

You have charged me to let my light shine.

I confess, I have not been Your best witness. I've hidden my light and operated in my own power. Forgive me, Lord. I seek to be united with You—consumed by You—for I recognize that apart from You, I can do nothing. Amen.

WORD OF LIFE

$$\infty$$

*That which was from the beginning. . .
concerning the word of life. . .[we] proclaim to you.*
1 JOHN 1:1–2 ESV

Jesus, You are the life-giving Word. The need of a lost world is to know You. The business of believers is to tell Your wonderful story. . .paint the picture. . .live the life. . . sow the seed. But sometimes my words and my life don't match up. Sometimes what I say betrays You.

Jesus, I'm sorry.

I ask that You continue to convict me when my mouth and Your truth are out of sync. I ask that You help me to speak Your words, and not my own. I ask, as the psalmist did, that You set a guard over my mouth and keep watch over the door of my lips (Psalm 141:3). May You, O Word of Life, be the words of my life so that others might have life in You! Amen.

Yahweh My God (Jehovah-Elohim)

*Then I fell on my knees and spread out
my hands to Yahweh my God.*
EZRA 9:5 HCSB

Ezra's prayer of confession when he learned of Israel's sin of intermarrying with the pagan nations:

"My God, I am ashamed and embarrassed to lift my face toward You, my God, because our iniquities are higher than our heads and our guilt is as high as the heavens. Our guilt has been terrible from the days of our fathers until the present. Because of our iniquities we have been handed over. . .to the surrounding kings, and to the sword, captivity, plundering, and open shame, as it is today. But now, for a brief moment, grace has come from Yahweh our God to preserve a remnant for us and give us a stake in His holy place. . . .

LORD God of Israel, You are righteous, for we survive as a remnant today. Here we are before You with our guilt, though no one can stand in Your presence because of this." (Ezra 9:6–8, 15 HCSB)

THANKSGIVING

*. . .because gratitude is the
antidote to grumbling*

*Give thanks in all circumstances;
for this is the will of God in Christ Jesus for you.*
1 THESSALONIANS 5:18 ESV

ABLE

*Now to him who is able to do immeasurably
more than all we ask or imagine.*
EPHESIANS 3:20 NIV

God, I've had a front-row seat watching You work!
You've orchestrated details and moved people at precisely
the right time in precisely the right way. You've stopped
me from completing specific tasks, even though I was
bent on doing them, and You've catapulted me into
conversations I never anticipated. You've situated every
component with meticulous exactness—bringing about
a result too calculated to be coincidental. And I stand in
awe of You. I lift high Your holy name—for You are the
One who is Able to do immeasurably more than all we
ask or imagine!

Thank You for adding to Your already extensive inventory of answered prayers!

Thank You for allowing me to experience Your able-
ness. Amen.

The Almighty (El Shaddai)

❧

Can you fathom the depths of God
or discover the limits of the Almighty?
Job 11:7 hcsb

Almighty God, I am so grateful for You today! Grateful that You do not get overwhelmed. Grateful that nothing takes You by surprise. Grateful that You've got this! Because I do get overwhelmed. I'm caught off guard. And I *don't* have this!

Knowing You as the Almighty, powerful, in-control God gives great comfort and confidence. I'm comfortable resting in Your strong hands. I'm confident moving in Your will. For no one can fathom Your understanding or discover the limits of Your power. Your ways are higher than my ways, and Your thoughts deeper than my thoughts. What a grand place to find security—in You!

O God above all gods, You are worthy of all praise and thanksgiving! Amen.

Author of Eternal Salvation

*And having been perfected, He became the author
of eternal salvation to all who obey Him.*
HEBREWS 5:9 NKJV

God, I know how difficult it is to craft a story line, create a few characters, and weave together the details of dialogue and plot—all the while hoping the loose ends tie up cleanly rather than fray uncontrollably! Writing anything—whether it be fiction, poetry, a prayer, or a lesson—challenges my ability to calculate and coordinate components. But the thought of authoring something on an *eternal* scale doesn't even compute!

The fact that *before* the foundation of the world, You knew Christ (1 Peter 1:20), loved Him (John 17:24), chose us to be holy and blameless in Him (Ephesians 1:4), and prepared a kingdom to be inherited with Him (Matthew 25:34) shows that You operate in a realm unparalleled! You wrote the details of our salvation before You ever uttered the words "Let there be light." As a result, I am now walking in the light.

O great Author of Eternal Salvation, thank You for writing me into Your story and including my name in the Lamb's book of life! The end. (Amen!)

BALM OF GILEAD

⊶

Is there no balm in Gilead?
JEREMIAH 8:22 NIV

Father, I'm wounded. I'm hurt. Sometimes the pain is so deep that I wonder why You've allowed it or why You're not lifting it. But then I remember that You are my Balm. You are the One who comforts and soothes—taking me into Your everlasting arms and easing the ache of my heart. When Job went through so much seemingly senseless suffering, he uttered words that now resonate with me: "I had only heard about you before, but now I have seen you with my own eyes" (Job 42:5 NLT).

Because of my pain, Lord, I see You.

Because of this wound, Lord, I know Your comfort.

Thank You, sweet Balm of Gilead.

Amen.

The Beginning

[Jesus] is the beginning, the firstborn from the dead.
COLOSSIANS 1:18 NKJV

Because of You. . .I have life. I'm trying to let that sink in, Lord.

You are the cause of life—"Then God said, 'Let us make man in our image'" (Genesis 1:26 ESV).

You are the reason for life—"For to me to live is Christ" (Philippians 1:21 ESV).

You are the giver of life—"For God so loved the world, that he gave his only Son" (John 3:16 ESV).

You inaugurated new life because You are the Beginning, the Firstborn from the Dead. You rose from the dead, paving the way to life! Now there will be no end to this eternal life that I have through faith in You.

Thank You for causing me to live. Thank You for being my reason to live. And thank You for giving me life eternal. May I live to please You. Amen.

BREAD OF LIFE

⎯⎯⎯∞⎯⎯⎯

*"I am the bread of life," Jesus told them. "No one who
comes to Me will ever be hungry, and no one who
believes in Me will ever be thirsty again."*
JOHN 6:35 HCSB

Nourishment, sustenance
Given from above—
Satisfying longings
Through Your gift of love.

Bread of Life, I thank You
For filling up my soul;
I pray my only hunger
Is You—that is my goal.

The Carpenter

"Isn't this the carpenter?"
MARK 6:3 HCSB

Jesus, it's good to know You as the Carpenter. I can picture You working pieces of wood—planing, sanding, and crafting them into functional and beautiful items. You had the ability to look at something knotty and misshapen and see the potential within, and with hammer in hand, You brought it to fruition.

Jesus, it's good to know You as my Carpenter. You looked at me—with all my knotty faults and misshapen flaws—and You saw a new creation. Through the nails in Your hands, You made something beautiful of my life.

Jesus, my Carpenter, You began a good work in me, and I thank You that You will bring it to completion on the day of Christ! Amen.

Counselor

For unto us a child is born, unto us a son is given. . .
and his name shall be called. . .Counsellor.
ISAIAH 9:6 KJV

O God, I'm frustrated! Today counselors give their latest research and findings as if they're groundbreaking. Then, based on their conclusions, they give advice as if it is novel. What frustrates me is that their findings aren't that groundbreaking! And their advice isn't that novel! As a matter of fact, I've read about these issues in the Bible. Ecclesiastes tells me that "there is nothing new under the sun" (Ecclesiastes 1:9 ESV) and that the end of the matter is to "fear God and keep his commandments" (Ecclesiastes 12:13 ESV).

So, Lord, I'm continually seeing that Your commandments are enough—by them You give understanding and wisdom. The psalmist even said, "They are my counselors" (Psalm 119:24 ESV). Lord Jesus, the Word, all-knowing Counselor, may I listen to You over and above the so-called experts. After all, Your Word has provided *everything* we need pertaining to life and godliness! For that, I thank You. Amen.

The Daysman

Neither is there any daysman betwixt us,
that might lay his hand upon us both.
Job 9:33 KJV

Lord, I don't think about Your return often enough. I rarely think about each of us standing before You on the day of reckoning. But whether I think about it or not, the truth remains—a day of reckoning is coming. You are coming.

I recognize that on that day, by all justice, I should hear a sentence that my sins deserve. If left to my own merit, a guilty verdict would be my lot. But You, my Daysman, will stand and speak for me. You, my mediator and arbitrator, have given me cause to turn my guilt into gladness—my sentence into celebration! How can I not worship You? How can I neglect to live in the light of this gift?

Thank You for reminding me of who You are and what You've done. Thank You for being my Daysman. Amen.

The Door of the Sheep

—∞∞—

So Jesus again said to them,
"Truly, truly, I say to you, I am the door of the sheep."
JOHN 10:7 ESV

"I am the door of the sheep." Lord, what a lesson in contrast. For You are I Am—the almighty, eternal, self-sufficient God! Yet You have made Yourself the Door of the Sheep—a position requiring humility and sacrifice. It is through You, and You alone, that we gain access to the Father. It is because of You we can rest, knowing we are protected from the enemy. Thank You for including me in Your flock. Thank You for allowing me to rest. Let me press into You today, safe and secure in Your love. Amen.

Faithful

"Know therefore that the Lord your God is God, the faithful God who keeps covenant and steadfast love with those who love him and keep his commandments, to a thousand generations."
Deuteronomy 7:9 esv

Lord, I've been praying and praying for You to bring help into a specific situation in my life. It seemed rather desperate and hopeless, and I wondered how You would work it out. But You did! You brought just the right people at just the right time! I'm overwhelmed with gratitude.

Faithful—it's what You are. It's who You are—to the very core! Trustworthy, dependable, steadfast, and consistent. Thank You for hearing my prayer and answering it beyond all I could ever ask or imagine. Thank You for being true. Thank You for being You—the Faithful God! Amen.

FATHER

---

*"I will be a Father to you, and you will be my sons
and daughters, says the Lord Almighty."*
2 CORINTHIANS 6:18 NIV

Father, Jesus taught us to pray to You. He began by
lifting high Your name, rendering it as holy, separate—
standing apart from all others. Lord, as our Father,
You do just that—You stand apart, surpassing all other
fathers. You set the standard. I'm not diminishing the
wonderful dad You gave me; in fact, I thank You and
praise You for the gift he has been in my life. I know
some who struggle in their relationship with their dads.
I pray for them, in particular, but ask that You help us
all to grasp this intimate dimension of our relationship
with You.

Lord, I am so grateful You are my Father! For You
are faithful, kind, trustworthy, and forgiving. You provide,
protect, defend, and preserve. You give instruction and
wise counsel. You are just, merciful, and gracious. You are
the giver of good and perfect gifts. You lavish us with
love. You are always there. And. . .You have chosen us—
adopted us as Your own!

I am Your child—You are my Daddy! In Your arms I
find all that I need. I love You. Amen.

THE FINISHER OF FAITH

Looking unto Jesus, the author and finisher of our faith.
HEBREWS 12:2 NKJV

Jesus, I thank You that You are the Finisher of my faith! You recognized the work that needed to be done because of my sin and set about to fix it. You authored the plan, and You accomplished it. For the joy set before You, You endured the cross, despised the shame, and sat down at the right hand of God in victory! If You had not endured, Jesus, I would be without hope.

But You did.

So now I possess an abundance of hope—a confident expectation that You who began a good work in me will be faithful to complete it, and will present me complete on the day of Christ!

Hallelujah! What a Savior! Thank You, Jesus my Lord! Amen.

A Friend Who Sticks Closer Than a Brother

⌇⌇⌇

A man of many companions may come to ruin,
but there is a friend who sticks closer than a brother.
Proverbs 18:24 esv

Jesus, I'm in a season of life that's lonely. Some days I handle it well; other days—not so much. I long for fellowship. I desire companionship. I need friendship. But it's been in this quiet struggle that I've learned to call You Friend, for in the stillness and seeming emptiness I've heard Your voice and felt Your love. What a blessing!

Thank You, Jesus, for being my Friend. Thank You for always, *always* being available to listen. Thank You for always, *always* being present when I call. And thank You for always, *always* loving me—no matter what! You are the Friend Who Sticks Closer Than a Brother, and I am the grateful companion. I love You, dear Friend. Amen.

GIVER OF EVERY GOOD GIFT

Every good gift and every perfect gift is from above,
coming down from the Father of lights.
JAMES 1:17 ESV

Father, I am filled with gratitude! I woke up this morning, all snuggled under the warmth of my comforter. My eyes saw the sunlight streaming through the windows. My ears heard the sound of the dog's paws on the hardwood floors. My husband gave me a kiss as he left for work. I had options for breakfast, warm water in my shower, things on my to-do list, and a car with which I could run errands. I received a funny text from my daughter, an email from my publisher, and a phone call from a friend.

Thank You for the gifts You give every day—from run-of-the mill household chores to extraordinary opportunities to serve You! You are the Giver of Every Good Gift. May I live in that awareness. I pray this in the name of the perfect gift You gave, Jesus Christ. Amen.

GLORIOUS FATHER

———— ∞ ————

I keep asking that the God of our Lord Jesus Christ,
the glorious Father, may give you the Spirit of wisdom
and revelation, so that you may know him better.
EPHESIANS 1:17 NIV

Paul's prayer of thanksgiving for the Ephesians:

"For this reason, ever since I heard about your faith in
the Lord Jesus and your love for all God's people, I have
not stopped giving thanks for you, remembering you in
my prayers. I keep asking that the God of our Lord Jesus
Christ, the glorious Father, may give you the Spirit of
wisdom and revelation, so that you may know him better.
I pray that the eyes of your heart may be enlightened in
order that you may know the hope to which he has called
you, the riches of his glorious inheritance in his holy people, and his incomparably great power for us who believe."
(Ephesians 1:15–19 NIV)

God of All Comfort

Praise the God and Father of our Lord Jesus Christ,
the Father of mercies and the God of all comfort.
2 Corinthians 1:3 hcsb

God, I praise You for being a God who comforts. You come alongside us in our sorrows, struggles, and pain, lending support and strengthening us in our weakness. I can look back over my life and pinpoint times when You were the One holding me up—because without You, I most certainly would have collapsed. I can remember specific instances when it was Your peace that soothed my aching heart—for the peace You offer passes all understanding.

Lord, I know Your Holy Spirit resides in me. I know it is through Him that You work in my life. Thank You for such a precious and needed gift—Your Spirit. He helps, He guides, He comes alongside, providing comfort from You, my Creator and Sustainer—my God of All Comfort. Amen.

THE GOD WHO SEES
(EL ROI)

⟨∞⟩

So she called the LORD who spoke to her:
The God Who Sees, for she said, "In this place,
have I actually seen the One who sees me?"
GENESIS 16:13 HCSB

Father God, I'm feeling invisible lately. Our society is so distracted with busyness that we've forgotten how to weep with those who weep and rejoice with those who rejoice! I'm experiencing both ends of that spectrum—celebrating great things You are doing in my life and ministry, but also struggling with trials that have brought me low. I desperately want someone to notice—but it seems everyone is too busy, caught up in their own trials and triumphs.

But that's when I remember that You are the God Who Sees! You see and know every detail of my life—every hurt and hallelujah of my heart. I don't need to seek out someone to pat me on the back or lend a shoulder to cry on, for You see and You know and You are there to hear my stories. Thank You, God, for seeing me. And thank You for allowing me to see You. Amen.

Good Master

Good Master, what shall I do that I may inherit eternal life?
MARK 10:17 KJV

"What shall I do?" Lord, this question resonates with many because we're doers. But if we contemplate our motivation, often we're convicted. *Doing* is a theme of the religious. *Earning* eternal life is a pretense of the pious. Following rules and marking off checklists gives a false sense that we play a part in salvation. And I've played no part—I've had no role—and here's why: "There is no one righteous, not even one" (Romans 3:10 NIV).

But You, Good Master, have released me from the chains of religion, opening the doors to freedom. You've shown me that it's not about following laws; it's about following *You*!

Thank You that I don't have to be fettered by legalism—instead, I am freed by love.

Thank You that You did the work on the cross—and now I can rest in Your grace.

Amen.

GUARANTOR

——∞——

This makes Jesus the guarantor of a better covenant.
HEBREWS 7:22 ESV

Lord, life is filled with uncertainties, situations where we lack assurance. We fret and fear, worry and wonder—all of which cause us to lose sleep, waste time, and miss the mark of trust that You've set for us. But You've shared a name, revealing an aspect of Your character that we can bank on—for You are our Guarantor. You are our security. Our bondsman. Our confidence. We can draw out drafts on the bank of heaven knowing You have pledged Yourself as our security.

Thank You that when my faith wavers, I can run to You, my Guarantor.

Thank You that I can count on You to come through—always. Amen.

Head above All

⬥

*"Yours is the kingdom, O Lord,
and you are exalted as head above all."*
1 Chronicles 29:11 esv

David's prayer of thanksgiving when the people gave a freewill offering for the house of the Lord:

"Blessed are you, O Lord, the God of Israel our father, forever and ever. Yours, O Lord, is the greatness and the power and the glory and the victory and the majesty, for all that is in the heavens and in the earth is yours. Yours is the kingdom, O Lord, and you are exalted as head above all. Both riches and honor come from you, and you rule over all. In your hand are power and might, and in your hand it is to make great and to give strength to all. And now we thank you, our God, and praise your glorious name.

"But who am I, and what is my people, that we should be able thus to offer willingly? For all things come from you, and of your own have we given you. . . . O Lord our God, all this abundance that we have provided for building you a house for your holy name comes from your hand and is all your own." (1 Chronicles 29:10–14, 16 esv)

A Hiding Place from the Wind

———— ∞ ————

A man will be as a hiding place from the wind.
Isaiah 32:2 NKJV

Father God, there's a movie about a three-thousand-mile horse race across the Arabian Desert. In one scene, a fierce sandstorm sweeps across the landscape. The rider forces his horse into an all-out gallop, attempting to outrun the storm, but to no avail. When it seems the massive cloud of dust will engulf him, he sees an outpost, and just as the sand begins to overtake him and his horse, they run into the shelter, escaping a sure death.

Lord, when I hear this name, a Hiding Place from the Wind, I picture this movie scene. It's a great reminder that You are my shelter! Sometimes the sandstorms of life are swirling about, nearly suffocating me. And just when I think I cannot handle it anymore, You provide exactly what I need—a Hiding Place in You. Thank You for being there. Thank You for allowing me to run to You when the winds of life howl. In Jesus' name I pray, amen.

I Am
(Jehovah/Yahweh)

———— ∞ ————

Jesus said to them, "Most assuredly,
I say to you, before Abraham was, I Am."
JOHN 8:58 NKJV

You are I Am. If I'm honest, I don't fully get that name. So I pray You will help me understand it more. . .understand You more. But I do recognize this name tells me something crucial about You—You exist. You always have and always will. This name tells me You will be there, present and constant in my life. It tells me You know the end from the beginning, which is comforting since so many days I don't know which end is up! Thank You, great I Am, that I can know You aren't going anywhere but that You Are in my every moment. Amen.

INDESCRIBABLE GIFT

∞

Thanks be to God for His indescribable gift.
2 CORINTHIANS 9:15 HCSB

Lord, I've been blessed to receive some pretty amazing gifts. I'm sure You remember when my husband picked me up from a conference in a brand-new car as a gift for our twentieth wedding anniversary! Talk about exciting! But that was several years ago. . .and now, as You know, the car has been driven over a hundred thousand miles, has stains on the upholstery, rust on the body, and makes noises it's not supposed to make. Kind of sums up the way of most gifts, doesn't it?

But You have outgiven every possible gift ever known! The gift of Jesus Christ to the world is incomparable! There is no treasure greater, and nothing more valuable!

He is Indescribable.

Inexpressible.

Too wonderful for words.

So when my words fail, I pray You will find my attitude and actions filled with never-ending thankfulness. You are the giver of every good and perfect gift, but You topped them all by giving Your only begotten Son for a sinner like me. Thank You, Lord! Amen.

Jealous
(Qanna)

⎯⎯ ∞∞ ⎯⎯

"You must worship no other gods, for the LORD,
whose very name is Jealous, is a God who is jealous
about his relationship with you."
Exodus 34:14 NLT

Lord, I heard someone railing against You—criticizing You for being a jealous God. They said that was not the kind of God they wanted; rather, they desired a loving God. They wanted to handcraft the attributes of their god—making a "have it your way," cafeteria kind of god. A man-made god.

But I see Your jealousy differently. I understand that You are not jealous *of* me, but You're jealous *for* me. Ironically, this jealousy *is* loving. You see me and want to be with me. You desire my highest good, and that highest good happens to be You. You are the highest God—not made with human hands or crafted by human thought, but eternal, compassionate, holy, just, and faithful. You love me tenderly and give of Yourself completely, so asking me to respond with simple loyalty seems a bit one-sided.

Thank You for Your lopsided love, Lord. Thank You for being jealous for me. Amen.

THE LAMB WHO WAS SLAIN

*And all who dwell on earth will worship it [the beast],
everyone whose name has not been written before the
foundation of the world in the book of life
of the Lamb who was slain.*
REVELATION 13:8 ESV

Jesus, You are the animal sacrificed in the Garden of Eden, providing skins for Adam's and Eve's covering. You are the ram caught in the thicket, a substitute for young Isaac when Abraham went to offer him on the altar. You are the animal cut in two during the covenant ceremony, shedding Your blood so mine could be spared. You are the Passover Lamb, whose blood protects from the death angel. Jesus, You are the Lamb of God who takes away the sins of the world. And You are the One who was destined for death before the foundation of the world was laid.

As the writer of Hebrews wrote, "Without the shedding of blood there is no forgiveness of sins" (9:22 ESV). How meager a mere thank-You sounds in relation to the cost of Your gift. But nonetheless I will utter it...no, *I will shout it*, for You are the Lamb Who Was Slain for me! *Thank You, Jesus!* Amen.

The Lifter of My Head

※

But you, O LORD, are a shield about me,
my glory, and the lifter of my head.
PSALM 3:3 ESV

Father God, today has been hard. I'm tired. I'm worn down. I'm weary. My body betrays me, and I'm sick of feeling sick. My head hurts—it's heavy—and I'm sad and discouraged. I know in Your Word the apostle Paul speaks about the thorn in his flesh, and although he doesn't identify it, I'm *convinced* it must have been migraines— because those have most definitely been my thorn. And like Paul, I've prayed and prayed and prayed for You to remove this thorn—to take away this chronic suffering. Yet it remains.

But this I know: You are the Lifter of My Head; You are the strength in my weakness. Most gladly, therefore, will I glory in my weakness, that Your power may be displayed in me. As You lift my head, Lord, I thank You for using this weakness to strengthen my dependence on You. Amen.

The Lord
(Jehovah)

⌘

*Then on that day David first appointed that thanksgiving
be sung to the Lord by Asaph and his brothers.*
1 Chronicles 16:7 esv

David's song of thanksgiving when the ark was brought
back to Jerusalem:

> Oh give thanks to the Lord; call upon his name;
>> make known his deeds among the peoples!
> Sing to him, sing praises to him;
>> tell of all his wondrous works!
> Glory in his holy name;
>> let the hearts of those who seek the Lord
>> rejoice!
> Seek the Lord and his strength;
>> seek his presence continually!
> Remember the wondrous works that he has done,
>> his miracles and the judgments he uttered.
>> (1 Chronicles 16:8–12 esv)

LORD JEHOVAH

∞

"Hear, O Israel! The LORD is our God, the LORD is one!"
DEUTERONOMY 6:4 NASB

Father, Son, and Holy Spirit—God in community—
You are God who has plurality, yet You are one. Your
triune, united character reveals the value You place on
relationship. So today I thank You for the relationships
You have given me, especially the ones in my inner
circle—my family.

Thank You for creating family. Thank You that family
gives us a place to belong, a tribe to rest in and wrestle
with—people who privately know your every weakness
yet are the first to boast about your strengths to the world.
Thank You for the inside jokes, facades stripped bare, and
insignificant moments that turn into priceless memories.
Thank You for the ups and downs, highs and lows, laughter, tears, and reassuring knowledge that we are one. Lord
Jehovah, thank You for providing the model of unity.
Thank You for being our relational God. Amen.

The Lord My Rock
(Jehovah-Tsuri)

⸻◦◦◦⸻

May the LORD, my rock, be praised, who trains my hands for battle and my fingers for warfare.
PSALM 144:1 HCSB

Who is steadfast, faithful, enduring, and strong? Who is solid, stable, permanent, and mighty? Is it not You, O Lord My Rock?

Thank You for being my footing—when the earth gives way.

Thank You for being my fortress—when the enemy attacks.

Thank You for being my foundation—when events overwhelm.

You are the Rock of Ages, cleft for me! And I will hide myself in Thee! Amen.

THE LORD WILL PROVIDE
(JEHOVAH-JIREH)

━━━━━∞∞∞━━━━━

*So Abraham called the name of that place,
"The LORD will provide"; as it is said to this day,
"On the mount of the LORD it shall be provided."*
GENESIS 22:14 ESV

Jehovah-Jireh, You are the God Who Provides. Thank You for all Your blessings, which are exceedingly, abundantly more than we could ever ask or imagine! Thank You for forgiveness and faith, laughter and love, family, friends, food, shelter, work, rest, and play. Thank You for our senses that allow us to feel, hear, smell, taste, and see that You're a good, good Father.

Most of all, Lord, we praise You for providing Jesus, the Lamb of sacrifice. Without Him, our lives would be hopeless. . .but because of Your provision, we can live in constant, confident expectancy.

I love You, Lord—not because of all You give, but because of who You are. Amen.

My Help
(Ezrah)

∞

God is our refuge and strength, a very present help in trouble.
PSALM 46:1 ESV

My son called me today, Lord. His travel plans fell through, and he desperately needed my help. As if I had nothing on my agenda, I quickly and eagerly jumped in the car to take him where he needed to go. We spent three precious hours together, and I found myself oddly grateful for his less than optimal circumstances. His dependence on me allowed us to spend one-on-one time together—time we don't get anymore since he moved away.

Reflecting on it, I realize it's not unlike my relationship with You. How I often make my own plans that take me away from You. How the less than optimal circumstances are the catalyst for some of our sweetest times together. How I know, no matter the time of day, You are there—always available, as if You have nothing else on Your agenda!

Thank You for being my Help, dear Father. Amen.

My Shepherd
(Jehovah-Raah)

The LORD is my shepherd, I lack nothing.
PSALM 23:1 NIV

Being likened to sheep is definitely *not* a compliment, Lord! Sheep are timid and fearful, easily distracted, weak, vulnerable, and generally not too bright. They need constant care and attention and can be extremely stubborn. They have a mob mentality and follow the flock even at their own detriment. They require guidance to eat, sleep, lie down, and rest. In other words, they're needy!

So am I. Needy, that is. That's why I need You most. Amazingly, You have a way of meeting every need. In You I lack nothing. In You I am blessed with every spiritual blessing in the heavenly realms. In You I have all I need. Thank You, dear Shepherd. Amen.

My Strength and My Song

⚛⚛⚛

*"Behold, God is my salvation; I will trust, and will not
be afraid; for the LORD GOD is my strength and
my song, and he has become my salvation."*
ISAIAH 12:2 ESV

Lord God, I must admit that fear cripples me at times,
and lately I've been paralyzed by it. I've been so focused
on the what-ifs—completely losing sight of You, the Who
Is! Thank You for the psalmist who reminds me that. . .

> *God* is my Salvation—and I can trust in Him.
> *God* is my Strength—and I do not have to be afraid.
> *God* is my Song—and singing of Him sets me free.

Lord, may my song be music to Your ears today—
even if a little out of tune. Amen.

An Offering

*And walk in love, as Christ also has loved us and given
Himself for us, an offering and a sacrifice to
God for a sweet-smelling aroma.*
EPHESIANS 5:2 NKJV

Jesus, not only did You talk the talk, but You walked the walk. On that last night with Your disciples, before You were crucified, You said, "Greater love has no one than this, than to lay down one's life for his friends" (John 15:13 NKJV).

You said, "This is how much I love you."
Then You spread out Your arms and died in my place.
Thank You for showing me what real love looks like.
Thank You for being my Offering. Amen.

The One I Love

I will arise now and go about the city,
through the streets and the plazas. I will seek the one I love.
Song of Solomon 3:2 hcsb

Lord, You loved me first,
While I wallowed in my sins.
Unworthy—that's me.

Lord, I love You now,
Accepting Your gracious gift.
Redeemed—I am free!

OUR HOPE

Paul, an apostle of Jesus Christ, by the commandment of God our Savior and the Lord Jesus Christ, our hope.
1 TIMOTHY 1:1 NKJV

Jesus, thank You for being my Hope. Thank You for giving me confidence that the promises written in Your Word *will* come to fruition—salvation from sin's penalty, freedom from sin's power, and ultimately the removal of sin's presence! Thank You that these are not the "I hope it happens, we've got a pretty good shot at it" kind of promises. But because You sealed the deal with Your own blood, I can know they are a sure thing!

I can wholly and completely trust in Your name, Lord Jesus, for my hope is built on nothing less than Jesus' blood and righteousness! Amen.

Our Lawgiver

For the LORD is our Judge, the LORD is our lawgiver,
the LORD is our King. He will save us.
ISAIAH 33:22 HCSB

Lord, thank You for being our Lawgiver. Your law brings order out of chaos. It corrals us and keeps us safe. Your law shows us our shortcomings—ultimately revealing our need for a Savior. You know us and understand our needs, so You made the law for us with infinite tenderness and love. Thank You for giving us Jesus Christ, who fulfilled that same law. Where I fell short, Jesus stepped in.

Lord, thank You for empowering me through Your Spirit to walk according to Your standards. May You know my love for You through my actions, for Your Word says, "The one who has My commands and keeps them is the one who loves Me" (John 14:21 HCSB). Amen.

PROVIDER

※

*Instruct those who are rich in the present age not to be arrogant
or to set their hope on the uncertainty of wealth, but on God,
who richly provides us with all things to enjoy.*
1 TIMOTHY 6:17 HCSB

Lord, there are sheets to change—which means I have loved ones under my roof. There is laundry to do—which means we have clothing to wear. I have a meal to cook—which means we are not lacking for food. There are phone calls to return—which means I have friendships. There's a deadline looming—which means I have a job. There's a lesson to prepare—which means I have the opportunity to share Your good news! Lord, I am blessed!

Thank You for providing these things and so much more! I am rich because of Your lavish love. Amen.

Rain upon Mown Grass

———∞———

May he be like rain that falls on the mown grass,
like showers that water the earth!
PSALM 72:6 ESV

Parched and dry—thirsty.
Rain falls and waters the earth.
You refresh my soul.

Redeemer (Ga'al)

"The Redeemer will come to Jerusalem to buy back those in Israel who have turned from their sins," says the LORD.
ISAIAH 59:20 NLT

Dear Lord, I play the comparison game too often—and find myself losing. When I look around, I see smarter, thinner, prettier, and more talented people than me. Women who are better at being a mom, a wife, and a friend. And those who are worthier to be called Your child. I don't measure up.

But right now, I want to thank You for reminding me that You use a different lens when You look at me. You see someone worthwhile—someone worth a great price! Thank You, my Redeemer, for buying me—flaws and all—and making me valuable through the precious blood of Jesus. Amen.

Rewarder

And without faith it is impossible to please Him,
for he who comes to God must believe that He is
and that He is a rewarder of those who seek Him.
Hebrews 11:6 nasb

Dear God,

I believe You are.

I believe You exist.

I believe there is no one higher—no one greater.

I believe all of heaven and earth are under Your authority.

I believe You are a good God, and Your goodness allows me to approach You.

I believe You are a loving God, and Your love compels me to seek You.

I believe You want the highest and the best for me—which translates into a deep relationship with You.

God, as I seek You, as I know You more—I'm finding You are the Rewarder. But more than that, You are *the* reward! Thank You for being my very great reward. Amen.

SANCTIFICATION
(JEHOVAH-MEKODDISHKEM)

⟨⟨⟨∞⟩⟩⟩

And because of him you are in Christ Jesus,
who became to us wisdom from God,
righteousness and sanctification and redemption.
1 CORINTHIANS 1:30 ESV

Lord, You call me to be set apart—holy. You command that I be different—uncommon. I recognize that in and of myself, it's just not possible—for I'm blemished, full of faults, and my flesh prevails. I end up looking like the world, and Your difference goes undetected.

But all is not lost—I am not lost! No, I have been saved. I'm secure. I'm set apart. I'm holy. Like a dirty old jacket, I've taken off the old self and put on Your righteousness! I am clothed in Christ! As I decrease and fully submit to You, I will not blend in with the world. Distinct, set apart, and uncommon for Christ—because of Christ!

Jesus, You are my Sanctification. You are my difference maker. It is You I praise! Amen.

Sanctuary (Miqdash)

⎯⎯⎯⎯⎯ ∞ ⎯⎯⎯⎯⎯

*"Therefore, tell the exiles, 'This is what the Sovereign LORD
says: Although I have scattered you in the countries of the
world, I will be a sanctuary to you during your time in exile.'"*
EZEKIEL 11:16 NLT

Lord, like the Israelites in Babylon, I'm a foreigner in a
foreign land. This place is not my home. I yearn for the
comfort of belonging. To know You as my Sanctuary,
then, softens that ache. As my Sanctuary, You provide a
place to center my mind on Your truth, take a deep breath
and feel Your calm, align my will with Yours, and worship
unhindered.

Thank You for being my Sanctuary—hiding me from
all earth's eyes and quieting me from all earth's clamor.
Amen.

Seed of the Woman

*"And I will put enmity between you and the woman,
and between your seed and her Seed; He shall bruise
your head, and you shall bruise His heel."*
GENESIS 3:15 NKJV

To be God of all creation and then humble Yourself to be birthed by that same creation is difficult to fathom. But then again, You are the God who shatters paradigms—upending norms and removing constraints. You became like me so I might have a relationship with You. You took on my sin so I might be clothed in Your righteousness. You made a way for restoration by exchanging Your glory for my shame. Jesus, Your actions shout Your love—every gesture declaring that You value me. And what makes something valuable? The price someone is willing to pay for it. Thank You for paying such an exorbitant price. Thank You for loving me lavishly. Now, may I live today in that understanding.

May I love today with that same mind-set. Amen.

Shiloh (Peacemaker)

———∞∞∞———

"The scepter shall not depart from Judah, nor the ruler's
staff from between his feet, until Shiloh comes,
and to him shall be the obedience of the peoples."
GENESIS 49:10 NASB

Dear God, You are a God who keeps Your word, faithfully fulfilling every detail—even the details we aren't looking for. You promised that Shiloh would come, and He did—Jesus Christ, the Messiah. He brought peace to those near and those far away. Peace to Your people Israel and to the entire Gentile world. Jesus, You bridged the gap, making two groups one. You make unity possible.

As I go about my day, keep me aware that You want all people to come to know You. Eliminate any hint of prejudice or pride in my life. May Your peace permeate my thoughts and actions—flowing out to a chaotic world that desperately needs You.

I thank You for bringing peace, just as You said You would do. Amen.

STONE OF ISRAEL

❦

But his bow remained in strength, and the arms of his hands were made strong by the hands of the Mighty God of Jacob (from there is the Shepherd, the Stone of Israel).
GENESIS 49:24 NKJV

O Stone of Israel, the chief cornerstone—You are the firm foundation, and as long as I build my life on You, I am assured it will stand. No trial, storm, difficulty, or circumstance can undermine Your strength. Finances, education, family, and health may seem sturdy for a while, but I have seen each of these so-called pillars crack, even crumble. But not You. You never give way. You are stable and secure. Thank You, God, for being my Rock, my sure footing. Amen.

Wisdom

———— ∞ ————

"I, Wisdom, live together with good judgment.
I know where to discover knowledge and discernment."
PROVERBS 8:12 NLT

Lord, it always amazes me when someone asks for my input—as if I have any advice to offer! I struggle and make a mess of my own decisions. But I know You are the source of all wisdom. You are the wellspring of knowledge. Your Word tells me that if anyone lacks wisdom, he should ask You, and You will dole it out generously. So I'm asking. And I pray I'll be able to direct my friend to You. Help us both to understand and know Your Word more so that we may live our lives in a manner that pleases You.

Thank You that we can come to You, the God of all wisdom. Amen.

Word of God

---∞---

He is clothed in a robe dipped in blood,
and the name by which he is called is The Word of God.
REVELATION 19:13 ESV

Thank You, Jesus Christ, for being the Word of God. Thank You for living out God's message of grace for all to read. Thank You for speaking words of life and truth. Thank You for preserving those words, making Yourself even more accessible to us.

Thank You for the Bible—the very breath of God. Thank You that through Your Word, I can know You— Your heart, Your thoughts, Your plan, Your purpose. Thank You for equipping me through Your Word—teaching, reproving, correcting, and training me in righteousness.

O God, may I forever exalt Your Word! And may You always find me rightly handling Your truth. Amen.

A Worm and Not a Man

But I am a worm and not a man,
scorned by men and despised by people.
PSALM 22:6 HCSB

Lord, it's crazy how mean we humans can be to one another. Sometimes I know the hurt happens because I'm being overly sensitive, but other times it's clear I'm the target—the target of ugly words and uglier attitudes. I find myself wanting to retaliate—come up with some clever quip that would put them in their place.

Rather than hurl words and cause wounds, I'm thankful I can talk with You about this, Lord. You get it, don't You? You understand. You, who bore scorn and reproach for me, suffered exponentially more than I ever will. And yet You didn't say anything ugly back! Oppressed and afflicted, You did not open Your mouth (Isaiah 53:7). You gave me an example to follow—of true grace and humility—extending forgiveness to the unlikely.

Thank You for listening, Lord, and thank You for bringing my actions and attitudes in closer alignment with Yours. Amen.

SUPPLICATION

. . .because He cares

Casting all your anxieties on him,
because he cares for you.
1 Peter 5:7 esv

The Alpha and Omega

*I am Alpha and Omega, the beginning and the ending,
saith the Lord, which is, and which was,
and which is to come, the Almighty.*
REVELATION 1:8 KJV

Lord God, when toddlers are frightened or overwhelmed by a situation, we pick them up and wrap them in our arms—totally encompassing their little bodies. Well, I'm completely overwhelmed right now, feeling like I'm free-falling. I read in scripture that You are the Alpha and Omega, the beginning and the end. That means You encompass *everything*! Surround me right now. Hold me in Your arms. Let me know the security that comes only from the One bigger than me. . .bigger than my situation. Amen.

THE AUTHOR OF FAITH

---∞---

Looking unto Jesus the author and finisher of our faith;
who for the joy that was set before him endured the cross,
despising the shame, and is set down at the
right hand of the throne of God.
HEBREWS 12:2 KJV

Jesus, history does matter. It gives us a clearer vantage point. But You keep showing me that *His* story matters more. *His* story—God's plan of rescue, motivated by love and given as a gift to the undeserving—matters for all of history. You have authored it with Your Word and finished it with victory over death. The last page of Your book looks like this: Satan is defeated and You reign!

Because I know Your story line, Lord, I pray today I'll live more boldly. Because I see You with a broader perspective, Lord, I surrender to You the pages of my life. Amen.

The Bridegroom

<hr>

*"In the middle of the night there was a shout:
'Here's the groom! Come out to meet him.'"*
MATTHEW 25:6 HCSB

Jesus, in New Testament times, the groom would spend the engagement period building and preparing a house for his bride. When his father felt his son had sufficiently prepared everything, he would send the son to the village to bring back his beloved bride.

Jesus, I know You are preparing a place for Your bride, the church. And because I know You as my Savior, I am part of Your church! You are coming again to take us where You are! I pray You will find us waiting with expectancy and prepared for You. Let us not get lazy. Let us not doubt or question Your return. Rather, may You find us eagerly anticipating the beautiful union of You, the Bridegroom, and Your bride, the church. Amen.

THE CAPTAIN OF THE
HOST OF THE LORD

⚬⚬⚬

*And he said, Nay; but as captain of the host
of the LORD am I now come.*
JOSHUA 5:14 KJV

Father God, the armies of Israel stood at the gateway of
the Promised Land. Their enemies loomed large—their
own skills and abilities lacking. Knowing their fear and
trepidation, You appeared to their leader, Joshua, assuring
him that nothing and no one could advance against Your
forces. The giants of the land would indeed submit to the
Captain of the Host of the Lord!

You are that same God today, and the giants I face
don't stand a chance against You! Lord, be my offense, my
defense, my power, and my confidence. As I bow in sub-
mission to You, take command and cause me to possess
the promises You have given! Amen.

CHRIST

❦

I want to know Christ—yes, to know the power of his
resurrection and participation in his sufferings,
becoming like him in his death.
PHILIPPIANS 3:10 NIV

Christ, as the apostle Paul prayed, so I am praying—I want
to know You more! I want to become more intimately
acquainted with all Your ways, knowing and perceiving
the remarkable wonders of Your person! I want to know
the power of Your resurrection residing within me through
Your Holy Spirit. I want to participate in Your sufferings,
being conformed to Your death through dying to self. May
I be crucified with You, Christ, so that it is no longer I who
live, but You who live in me!

It's a dangerous prayer, Jesus, but I believe there is no
higher calling than to know You. Help me to seek You
through prayer. . .through Your Word. . .through Your
presence. . .through Your Spirit. And when all is said and
done, may I be able to say with Paul, "I consider everything a loss because of the surpassing worth of knowing
Christ Jesus my Lord" (Philippians 3:8 NIV). Amen.

CREATOR
(ELOHIM)

———— ∞ ————

*"Bring all who claim me as their God, for I have made
them for my glory. It was I who created them."*
ISAIAH 43:7 NLT

God, Your Word tells me that You created me for Your
glory. What an incredible thought! You gave me a purpose
from the moment You began knitting me together in my
mother's womb. I don't have to wonder why You've placed
me here. All the days ordained for me were written in
Your book before one of them came to be—and each of
those days has been given *so that* You may be honored.

May I work *so that* Your name is lifted high.

May I interact with others *so that* they might see You.

May I talk and think *so that* You are pleased.

I pray that everything I do gives a proper estimate of
who You are—the God of all creation! Amen.

CREATOR
(ELOHIM)

∞

*When I think of all this, I fall to my knees and pray to the
Father, the Creator of everything in heaven and on earth.*
EPHESIANS 3:14–15 NLT

Paul's prayer for the believers in Ephesus:

"I pray that from his glorious, unlimited resources he
will empower you with inner strength through his Spirit.
Then Christ will make his home in your hearts as you
trust in him. Your roots will grow down into God's love
and keep you strong. And may you have the power to understand, as all God's people should, how wide, how long,
how high, and how deep his love is. May you experience
the love of Christ, though it is too great to understand
fully. Then you will be made complete with all the fullness of life and power that comes from God." (Ephesians
3:16–19 NLT)

A Crown of Glory

*In that day the LORD of hosts
will be a crown of glory.*
ISAIAH 28:5 ESV

Lord, I'm feeling compelled to pray for our husbands, sons, brothers, and fathers. Satan is working overtime in our society to undermine the role of men—emasculating and weakening them. So I pray for strength for our men—physical, emotional, and spiritual. I pray that they will be men after Your heart, Lord—dealing justly, loving mercy, and walking humbly with You. I pray they will be men of integrity—standing firm on Your truth—not regarding their reputation, but corroborating Your character. God, may they be like Jesus, Your Crown of Glory, giving the proper honor and attention to Your name! Amen.

FATHER

*"Pray, then, in this way:
'Our Father who is in heaven,
hallowed be Your name.' "*
MATTHEW 6:9 NASB

Our Father. What a privilege to come before You as one of Your children! I can know with certainty that I belong to You because Your Word tells me, "As many as received Him [Jesus Christ], to them He gave the right to become children of God, even to those who believe in His name" (John 1:12 NASB). And as Your child, I am an heir. What a thought! It's a rags-to-riches story line—a prince and the pauper fairy tale—only this isn't fiction. For You are King, and I am Your child. You have blessed me with every spiritual blessing in the heavenly places (Ephesians 1:3).

Father, let me live in that knowledge today—and let me seek out others to share with them this sweet relationship. Because I'm certain You want more children. I pray this in Your holy name. Amen.

Friend of Sinners

꩜

Behold. . .a friend of publicans and sinners.
Matthew 11:19 kjv

Loving people isn't easy, is it, Lord? Because people are sinners, and sin has consequences, and consequences get complicated. I admit that sometimes it scares me to get involved in the messes. Involvement takes time, effort, energy, emotion, and money. And sometimes I get cynical and hard-hearted. Sometimes it's just flat-out pride. Honestly, I don't want to be like that. I want to be like You, Jesus—a Friend of Sinners.

Lord, I pray for courage to overcome the fear of getting involved. I pray for compassion to guide my interactions with others. I pray for humility as I recognize my own mess that You willingly and lovingly stepped into.

I ask, through the power of Your Spirit, that I love people like You do—even when it gets messy. Amen.

GOD OF ALL COMFORT

Praise the God and Father of our Lord Jesus Christ,
the Father of mercies and the God of all comfort.
2 CORINTHIANS 1:3 HCSB

Father of Mercies, I pray for my friends experiencing great affliction and difficulty. They are weak, tired, and hurting. They are physically, emotionally, and spiritually drained. But Your name gives great hope—so I call upon that name right now! God of All Comfort, be the comfort my friends need. Wrap them in Your loving arms. Let them sense Your nearness. Give them rest and relief. . .allow them a respite from the pain and struggle.

And, Lord, prompt Your people to be Your hands and feet to them. Show us how we might meet their needs and offer support. I know I have been the recipient of Your comfort and care—now may I move in that same rhythm. Amen.

GOD OF HEAVEN
(ELOHIM SHAMAYIM)

⌘

When I heard this, I sat down and wept. In fact,
for days I mourned, fasted, and prayed to the God of heaven.
NEHEMIAH 1:4 NLT

The prayer of Nehemiah before he asked King Artaxerxes (his boss) if he could go to Jerusalem to help his people rebuild the wall:

"O LORD, God of heaven, the great and awesome God who keeps his covenant of unfailing love with those who love him and obey his commands, listen to my prayer! Look down and see me praying night and day for your people Israel. I confess that we have sinned against you. Yes, even my own family and I have sinned! We have sinned terribly by not obeying the commands, decrees, and regulations that you gave us through your servant Moses. . . .

"The people you rescued by your great power and strong hand are your servants. O Lord, please hear my prayer! Listen to the prayers of those of us who delight in honoring you. Please grant me success today by making the king favorable to me. Put it into his heart to be kind to me." (Nehemiah 1:5–7, 10–11 NLT)

GOD OF OUR FATHERS

"O Lord, God of our fathers, are you not God in heaven?"
2 CHRONICLES 20:6 ESV

The prayer of Jehoshaphat upon hearing of an imminent attack from an enemy army:

"O Lord, God of our fathers, are you not God in heaven? You rule over all the kingdoms of the nations. In your hand are power and might, so that none is able to withstand you. Did you not, our God, drive out the inhabitants of this land before your people Israel, and give it forever to the descendants of Abraham your friend? And they have lived in it and have built for you in it a sanctuary for your name, saying, 'If disaster comes upon us, the sword, judgment, or pestilence, or famine, we will stand before this house and before you—for your name is in this house—and cry out to you in our affliction, and you will hear and save.'. . .O our God. . . we are powerless against this great horde that is coming against us. We do not know what to do, but our eyes are on you." (2 Chronicles 20:6–9, 12 ESV)

THE GOD WHO WORKS WONDERS

∞∞∞

You are the God who works wonders;
You have made known Your strength among the peoples.
PSALM 77:14 NASB

Almighty Father, You are the God Who Works Wonders! And I wonder. . .if I lived during the time of Moses, would I have believed it was You who changed the Nile to blood? If I knew the prophet Elijah, would I have acknowledged it was You who fed him bread and meat through the ravens? If my contemporaries included Shadrach, Meshach, and Abednego, would I have recognized You walking in the furnace with them? If I witnessed firsthand dead-for-four-days Lazarus coming out of the tomb—fully alive—would I have understood that Jesus generated the resurrection?

Lord, I recently participated in a baptism. I watched a young lady plunge into a watery grave and emerge with a fist pump and a "Hallelujah!" I *know* that You are the God Who Worked Wonders throughout the Old and New Testaments—and You are the God Who Works Wonders still today!

I believe, Lord. Help my unbelief. Amen.

GOOD SHEPHERD
(JEHOVAH-RAAH)

———— ⟨∞⟩ ————

"I am the good shepherd.
The good shepherd gives His life for the sheep."
JOHN 10:11 NKJV

Good Shepherd, I ask that You keep watch over my children. Supply comfort, ease, security, and safety for these kids who will forever have my heart. I ask that they have happiness, health, strong marriages, and good jobs. But I know that happiness and ease are not Your ultimate goals for them—holiness is Your highest design. Honestly, that's what I want for them, too, but I realize that sometimes it takes hurts and hardships to bring about that end.

This is why I am calling on You, my Good Shepherd—because the Good Shepherd gives His life for the sheep. I can count on You to care for, comfort, and protect, while doing that which is necessary to raise strong sheep.

Lord, I love these precious ones. . .but I know You love them more. Keep watch over them, I pray. Amen.

A Grain of Wheat

*And Jesus answered them, "The hour has come for
the Son of Man to be glorified. Truly, truly, I say to you,
unless a grain of wheat falls into the earth and dies,
it remains alone; but if it dies, it bears much fruit."*
JOHN 12:23–24 ESV

Jesus, I long to be more like You. This description of You
as a Grain of Wheat epitomizes what it takes. A grain
of wheat is so small, it can hardly be held between the
fingers without dropping it—yet it's associated with
Your glory! A grain of wheat requires death and burial in
order to bring forth fruit. And You, like a grain of wheat,
endured both. The result? A continual production of fruit!

So, Jesus, if I am to be more like You, I, too, must die—
die to self and die to this world. May I be about the business
of bringing You glory—bearing much fruit through Your
name, following Your example. Amen.

Head over All Things

God has put all things under the authority of Christ
and has made him head over all things for
the benefit of the church.
Ephesians 1:22 nlt

God, I love how You are a God of order and purpose. You placed Jesus Christ over all things for the benefit of the church. Your desire is to present the church to Him as a beautiful, radiant bride. As part of that church, I pray that I might add to Your bride's beauty by submitting to Christ as the Head.

When my own selfish desires and prideful ways rise up, I ask You to empower me to crucify them for Your glory.

When I try to usurp Your rightful place of authority, I ask You to humble me so that You might be exalted.

When I go outside the boundaries of Your plan, I ask You to reroute me for Your name's sake.

O Christ, Head over All Things, I submit myself to Your authority this day. Thank You for allowing me to be part of Your beloved bride. Amen.

THE HOLY ONE OF GOD

*"Why are you interfering with us, Jesus of Nazareth?
Have you come to destroy us? I know who
you are—the Holy One of God!"*
MARK 1:24 NLT

Jesus, this declaration—that You are the Holy One of God—came from the lips of one possessed by an unclean spirit. A spawn of Satan would seem an unlikely source to give testimony of Your glory. But truth cannot be denied or decried! If need be, You said even the rocks would cry out Your praise (Luke 19:40).

The convicting question is, as Your child, how much more should I be shouting this truth to a dark and dying world? Jesus, You are the Holy One of God who has power over Satan. You have set captives free, opened the eyes of the blind, made the deaf hear, and caused the lame to walk. I know You can open the mouth of this one who is sometimes mute. Loose my lips to declare Your praise! I don't want demonic forces or stones to do the job I should be clamoring to do. I pray this in Your powerful name, Jesus. Amen.

I Am
(Jehovah/Yahweh)

―――――∞∞∞―――――

But Moses protested, "If I go to the people of Israel and tell them,
'The God of your ancestors has sent me to you,' they will ask
me, 'What is his name?' Then what should I tell them?"
God replied to Moses, 'I Am Who I Am. Say this
to the people of Israel: I Am has sent me to you."
Exodus 3:13–14 nlt

What a name! I Am.

And since You are I Am, it must mean that I am not. When I put that into perspective, Lord, it's humbling, but freeing, too. You are the One in control, not me. I act like I'm in control, don't I—taking the reins and thinking I know best. But You are the One with the grand plan and a panoramic view, while I'm looking out at the scenery through a mere keyhole. Help me trust You more. After all, You Are God. I am not. Amen.

INTERCESSOR

And the Holy Spirit helps us in our weakness. For example, we don't know what God wants us to pray for. But the Holy Spirit prays for us with groanings that cannot be expressed in words.
ROMANS 8:26 NLT

Holy Spirit, we Christians seem to make You take a backseat in the Trinity. But You are God! I praise You for being God. I praise You for Your role in our world and in my life. How amazing to think that You, the Spirit of God, who knows the mind of God, dwell within me—leading, guiding, comforting, teaching, convicting, prompting, and praying for me.

Thank You for being my Intercessor. When I don't know what to say or how to pray, I can trust You to take my needs before the throne of grace! I pray that I would not grieve You. I pray that I would not quench You. Rather, I ask that You stir up Your fire within me to think, and move, and act in holy boldness.

I ask that I be conscious of Your presence in my moments—and rest in You as You intercede on my behalf. Amen.

KING OVER ALL THE EARTH
(MELEK)

━━━━━∞∞∞━━━━━

And the LORD will be king over all the earth.
ZECHARIAH 14:9 NASB

Lord, many political leaders and CEOs and people who have put themselves in positions of authority scoff at the idea of You. Conversations at coffee shops, comedic exchanges on TV, and dialogue among self-appointed pundits deny Your existence. And my gut reaction is like James and John's—that You rain down fire from heaven on them! But by knowing Your heart, even a little bit, I know my request must change—I ask You to open their eyes so that they might see You, the King over All the Earth. I ask that they might be saved by You, O gracious King of glory.

King over All the Earth, thank You for opening my eyes to You. May I be a herald to those near to You and those far away—a champion for Your cause! I pray I follow Your example, and not my gut, by showing love and giving grace to all people everywhere. Amen.

A Leader

⎯⎯⎯⎯ ∞ ⎯⎯⎯⎯

"See how I used him to display my power among the peoples.
I made him a leader among the nations."
ISAIAH 55:4 NLT

I love that You lead me, Lord! I love that You have a plan
far greater than anything I could map out for myself. I
love that You have a grander purpose not only for me, but
for all Your creation. I love that You are trustworthy—
Your track record proves it! And I love that You love
me—so I trust You completely.

Wherever You lead me today, may I follow willingly.

Whomever You bring my way, may I represent You
well.

Whatever circumstances You allow in my life, may I
walk through them for Your glory.

Amen.

Lily of the Valleys

"I am the rose of Sharon, the lily of the valleys."
Song of Solomon 2:1 NASB

The sweetest, fairest, most exquisite flower that the eye has seen is the lily of the valley—hidden except to eyes that seek it out. So are You, Lord. As I walk through the valleys, I pray that I seek You—for in the seeking, You promise I will find You! In the seeking, You promise there is great reward!

Lord, I believe that You exist. Lord, I draw near to You. Lord, may You be pleased with my seeking. Here's my heart, O Lord. It is wholly Yours. Amen.

LIVING GOD

*For they themselves report about us what kind of a reception
we had with you, and how you turned to God
from idols to serve a living and true God.*
1 THESSALONIANS 1:9 NASB

Lord, so many in our world are searching for truth but
have been deceived by Satan, the father of lies. They
have been duped into thinking that worshipping a dead
prophet or following a man-made idol will somehow
fill the God-shaped void in their lives. I pray for them,
Lord. I pray that the scales will fall from their eyes and
they will see You, the true and Living God! The God who
abolished death and brought life and immortality to light
through the Gospel (2 Timothy 1:10).

You are the God who cannot be constructed or
contained.

You are the God who lived and still lives today.

You are the God of truth who transforms lives.

You are living. You are active. You are God!

I pray the world will know You and be changed by
You. Amen.

The Living One

———— ✺ ————

*"I am the living one. I died, but look—I am alive forever
and ever! And I hold the keys of death and the grave."*
REVELATION 1:18 NLT

Jesus, living in this world hurts. We lose loved ones and
take issue with Your timing. We can't make sense of why
they are taken from us. We grieve and ache and long to
hold them again, or talk to them one more time, or see
their faces. And we question You.

In times like this, Lord, I pray You would help me
to know You as the Living One. Death took aim at You,
too—attempting to end Your rule and reign. But You
conquered death! You rose again! You are alive today and
forever!

Jesus, because of You, there is hope for an exchange—
the perishable for the imperishable; mortality for immortality. Because of You, I have a broader view and can
boldly declare, "O death, where is your victory? O death,
where is your sting?" (1 Corinthians 15:55 NLT).

And because of You, even in the midst of utter grief,
I can lift my arms and say. . .praise be to Jesus Christ, the
Living One!

THE LORD IS PEACE
(JEHOVAH-SHALOM)

❧

Then Gideon built an altar there to the LORD
and named it The LORD is Peace.
JUDGES 6:24 NASB

Lord, turmoil reigns in our world today. Conflict is a cancer. The idea of peace seems unreasonable. . . unattainable. Hatred among nations, races, and political parties prompts all manner of evil. Dissension, hostility, and discord continually metastasize, overtaking the uttermost parts of the earth, and close in on the confines of our own homes. The world desperately needs a cure!

My Yahweh Shalom, I pray You be that cure! You are the Lord our Peace—the source of all peace. We beg You to open our hearts that You might reign and rule. Let us understand that Your peace is grander than the mere absence of conflict—Your peace brings wholeness, completeness, wellness, and perfection. Lord, You have extended peace to us through Jesus, the Prince of Peace. I pray we will embrace His offering, surrendering our claim on conflict. For it is only in surrender that we will experience true shalom. Amen.

THE LORD MY BANNER
(JEHOVAH-NISSI)

※

And Moses built an altar and called the name of it,
The LORD Is My Banner, saying, "A hand upon the throne
of the LORD! The LORD will have war with
Amalek from generation to generation."
EXODUS 17:15–16 ESV

Lord, You are so true, so faithful, and so trustworthy. You are the One who made the way by providing the sacrifice of Jesus, Your Son whom You loved. You are the One who has prepared the plan, acted on that plan, and followed through with it. You've done it all, and yet all You ask of me is obedience to the perfect truth. And I'm learning that obedience is better than sacrifice, for had there been obedience, there would be no need for a sacrifice!

God, Amalek is at war. The flesh battles Your Spirit in me on a daily basis, and I live such a defeated life because I don't rally at Your standard. I pray for Your victory against the flesh this week. Help me to set my mind on things above and focus on You, Jehovah-Nissi—The Lord My Banner! Amen.

MASTER

And the Lord said, "Who then is the faithful and sensible steward, whom his master will put in charge of his servants, to give them their rations at the proper time?"
LUKE 12:42 NASB

Lord, as Master and owner of all things, You have entrusted to us the role of manager—asking that we faithfully steward all You have given. The apostle Paul wrote that it was his aim to please You (2 Corinthians 5:9). Lord, as Your steward, I also aim to please You.

I pray that I please You with my time, utilizing each moment, maintaining a kingdom mind-set.

I pray that I please You with my talent, releasing any fears or past failures that might hinder me from seizing opportunities You place in my path.

I pray that I please You with my treasure, knowing that even the cattle on a thousand hills belong to You. As You lead me to let go for Your glory, I pray I will do so with great expectations, knowing You have bigger blessings in store.

Lord, I pray You find me faithful. Master, I pray You will be pleased. Amen.

Most High
(El Elyon)

∽

"The Most High rules in the kingdom of men."
DANIEL 4:17 NKJV

Jesus, today I want to lift up our nation. Anxiety is high; morality is low. Safety is an issue and security elusive. It's easy to criticize and complain, and tempting to point fingers of blame, but You have commanded that we pray. So I lift up the leaders of our land to You. I ask that they be convicted to seek You. May they understand and know their position before You. I ask that they desire Your wisdom and humble themselves under Your mighty hand. May they lead in that wisdom, seeking the welfare of the nation. I pray that they execute justice in our land, honoring people of integrity and punishing evildoers. And I pray for unity. Political conflict and religious strife are soaring right now, and I ask that You draw people together in one accord.

Lord, You are the Most High God, setting up kings and deposing them. You are higher and mightier than any world leader, directing hearts as You will. So I pray Your will for our leaders, trusting You as You set in place the men and women who do Your bidding. Amen.

My Confidence

---∞---

For You are my hope, Lord GOD,
my confidence from my youth.
PSALM 71:5 HCSB

Father God, sometimes we put ourselves "out there" in ministry in a way that exposes us to others. Honestly, it's a little scary to open yourself to the potential of being cut down by nitpicking and criticism.

So I'm praying right now that You would be my Confidence! I give You my insecurities and trust You with the results. I know You have called me to step out of my comfort zone, so in obedience I'm taking those steps. Thank You for the apostle Paul's encouragement; he put things in perspective when he said, "For am I now seeking the approval of man, or of God? Or am I trying to please man? If I were still trying to please man, I would not be a servant of Christ" (Galatians 1:10 ESV). Lord, I want to please You, not man!

Father, thank You for calling me to serve You. Thank You for being my Confidence! Amen.

My Glory

But you, O Lord, are a shield around me;
you are my glory, the one who holds my head high.
PSALM 3:3 NLT

Lord, glory is Your holiness gone public. So if You are my Glory, that means Your holiness can be made evident through me! What a humbling thought. . .that You could use messed-up me to make Yourself known to the world.

Today I pray my desires and my will be crucified with You. Today I pray it is no longer I who live, but Christ living in me. And today I pray that the life I live will bring honor to You. May Your holiness go public in my family, through my work, in my community, and throughout my little world today because You are my Glory! Amen.

MY PRAISE

∞

I will bless the LORD at all times;
his praise shall continually be in my mouth.
PSALM 34:1 ESV

Lord, today is a new day. An original, never-to-be-repeated day. A day full of new mercies and fresh starts. There are hours and minutes and moments ahead filled with opportunities to praise You. I pray I make the most of these moments—not for my benefit, but for Your glory. Keep my heart humble, my eyes elevated, and my hands heavenward. Let me show my passion for Your name. Whatever the day holds, Lord, I am convinced that. . .

Circumstances cannot circumvent Your presence.

People will not prevent Your praise.

Worry won't weaken Your power.

Lord, may today be a showcase for Your name—for You are my Praise and no one is worthier than You! Amen.

Our Keeper

⌘

"While I was with them,
I kept them in your name,
which you have given me."
JOHN 17:12 ESV

Jesus, as children we pray, "Now I lay me down to sleep, I pray the Lord my soul to keep." Our childish minds don't grasp it, but praying for You to "keep" me is a powerful prayer! So now, as an adult, I ask again that You keep. . .

my feet from walking toward evil
my lips from speaking lies
my hands from idleness
my mind from things of the earth

Thank You, my Savior, for keeping me.

"Now all glory to God, who is able to keep you from falling away and will bring you with great joy into his glorious presence without a single fault" (Jude 1:24 NLT). Amen.

OUR POTTER

⌘

Yet you, LORD, are our Father. We are the clay,
you are the potter; we are all the work of your hand.
ISAIAH 64:8 NIV

Remold and remake.
Whatever's necessary,
I trust my Potter.

I'm a lump of clay;
You are the great artisan.
Shape me with Your hands.

THE OVERCOMER

⸺⸺ ∞ ⸺⸺

"I have overcome the world."
JOHN 16:33 NIV

Before He went to the cross, Jesus uttered these words: "I have overcome the world."

Before He endured unimaginable suffering, Jesus confidently declared, "I have overcome the world."

Before He hung on the cross, *before* He gave up His life, *before* He lay dead in the tomb, *before* He raised Himself from the dead—Jesus said, "I have overcome the world."

Why? Because You really had!

Lord, *before* I face the trials coming my way, the tribulations headed in my direction, and the tests that may rock my world, I pray You help me remember Your name—Overcomer! Why? Because You are! You have overcome the world! And in You I am ensured victory! Amen.

· PHYSICIAN

Jesus said to them, "Surely you will quote this proverb to me: 'Physician, heal yourself!'"
LUKE 4:23 NIV

Jesus, my daughter is sick and I need You to intervene! You are the mighty miracle worker. When You walked this earth You healed the sick, made the lame leap, the blind see, the deaf hear. You cast out demons and even raised the dead! I have no doubt You work miracles today, too—yet I seem to be missing them!

Open my eyes to see You. Keep reminding me that not only are You the Great Physician; You are the greatest. You healed the most fatal sickness of all—sin— through Your death, burial, and resurrection. Forgive me for doubting or questioning Your ways. Forgive me for not trusting You with my precious girl. She's precious to You, too. . .and so infinitely loved that You gave Your own life for her. O Jesus, the Greatest Physician, work Your miracles in her life. I trust You. Amen.

The Power of God

Christ the power of God.
1 Corinthians 1:24 NIV

Stronger than gale-force winds and mightier than a raging torrent is Your power, O Lord! Dynamic. Influential. Inherent. Overarching.

You work miracles. You move mountains. You calm storms. You give life. And the power You used to bring victory over Satan is the same power You have given me! So why do I live with such a defeated mind-set? Why do I allow Satan any foothold?

In the name of Jesus Christ—the Power of God—I declare victory today! I pray for victory over my thoughts, actions, interactions, and words. I pray for victory over the temptations that garner my attention. I pray that any strongholds Satan has over my family will be undone! I pray for all Your followers, that we may be emboldened to share Your good news and give others victory over sin. I pray for victory for Your church and Your people—that the gates of hell will not prevail! For You, Jesus, are the Power of God! Thank You that as Your child, I can plug into Your power and live victoriously. Amen.

Prophet Mighty in Deed and Word

And he said to them, "What things?" And they said to him,
"Concerning Jesus of Nazareth, a man who was a prophet
mighty in deed and word before God and all the people."
Luke 24:19 esv

O Jesus, Mighty Prophet, Your deeds and Your Word declare truth: You are the only Savior! As it was when You walked this earth, some accept that truth while others reject it. While coming face-to-face with You, the living God, some hate You, while others worship You. Regardless of our response—You are still God!

Mighty in life.

Mighty in death.

Mighty in resurrection.

Prophesying Your life, death, and resurrection long before they took place and establishing Your plan of salvation from the beginning, You have proclaimed Your might to all people over all time.

Lord, I pray I respond with continual awe and acceptance! Open my spiritual eyes, like You did for the disciples on the road to Emmaus. Deepen my understanding of Your deeds and Your Word. Intensify my faith for Your glory! Amen.

REFINER
(TSARAPH)

꩜

*"He will sit like a refiner of silver, burning away the dross.
He will purify the Levites, refining them like gold and silver,
so that they may once again offer acceptable
sacrifices to the LORD."*
MALACHI 3:3 NLT

This refining process stinks, Lord. Not in the smelly sort
of way, but in a way that hurts not with physical pain but
with a heavy heart. I'm facing uncertainties—and have
no idea where You are leading. I've been criticized, my
motives called into question—even as I'm pouring myself
out as an offering to You. And the waiting is wearying,
the doubting discouraging.

But this I know, that You are for us (Psalm 56:9)! You
are burning away the dross in my life so Your reflection
can be readily seen. If it takes more waiting and doubting
and criticizing and pouring out—then so be it, Lord. And
even though it stinks and hurts, I trust that You know
what You're doing to make me look more like Jesus.

O Refining God, have Your way with me. I trust You.
Amen.

Restorer

He restores my soul; He leads me in the paths
of righteousness for His name's sake.
PSALM 23:3 NKJV

Depleted. That's how I feel. It seems everyone needs something from me—and I'm running on empty. My emotions are high and my energy low, and I'm desperate for renewal. So, Lord, even as I sputter toward You, I do it with great expectancy, knowing You will refill and renew. You will breathe life back into my inner being. You are my Restorer. No one else—not my husband, children, family, or friends—can replenish like You. Nothing else—not medicine, sleeping, eating, withdrawing—can revive my soul like You. So I come to You, wait on You, and rest in Your capable hands. Restore me, Lord. Amen.

Ruler
(Mashal)

⋘

*"Bethlehem Ephrathah. . .out of you will come for me one
who will be ruler over Israel, whose origins are
from of old, from ancient times."*
Micah 5:2 niv

Jesus, all authority in heaven and on earth has been given to You. Yet I live under a false illusion that somehow I run my own little world. But Your Word says that as Your child, I've been crucified with You, and it is no longer I who live but You living in me.

So it seems once again I'm in need of a reality check—an inventory of areas that need crucified and put under Your authority. Areas such as:

My finances—everything is Yours, Lord; help me to hold loosely the things You've allowed me to steward.

My attitude—complaining and criticizing do not reflect Your rule in my life; help me give thanks in all circumstances today.

My relationships—You know I'm task oriented, Jesus, and relationships are hard for me; help me show love for You by loving others.

Rule and reign over my life today, Lord. I pray this in the name of Jesus, Ruler of heaven and earth! Amen.

A Shade from the Heat

For you have been. . .a shade from the heat.
ISAIAH 25:4 ESV

Father God, You ask us to remember those who are in prison and those who are mistreated, since we are all part of the body. So, Lord, I want to lift up my Christian brothers and sisters around the globe who are enduring severe persecution. Because they name You as Lord, they face brutal beatings, dismemberment, rape, imprisonment, and even death. Like Paul, they bear on their bodies the brand marks of Jesus Christ!

Lord, I know they have a crown of life awaiting them, an eternal reward. But while they remain here, I pray You give them comfort. Be their Shade, Father, a respite from the intense heat they are facing. Relieve their pain as only You can. Amen.

A Sharp Sword

⸺ ∞ ⸺

He made my words like a sharp sword.
ISAIAH 49:2 HCSB

Jesus, all throughout the Bible You are pictured as the Word of God—speaking words of peace, comfort, and power to Your people. But Your Word is also described as a Sharp Sword, a polished shaft—"cutting between soul and spirit, between joint and marrow. It exposes our innermost thoughts and desires" (Hebrews 4:12 NLT). Your Word is alive and powerful.

I ask that Your Word be alive in me—active in my life. Cut away the areas that hinder holiness. Use Your Sharp Sword like a scalpel, removing anything contrary to Christ. I pray You conform me to Your image through Your Word. . .and may I respond like Samuel: "Speak, LORD, your servant is listening" (1 Samuel 3:9 NLT). Amen.

A SHIELD

But You, LORD, are a shield around me,
my glory, and the One who lifts up my head.
PSALM 3:3 HCSB

Jesus, a spiritual battle rages today. Like most days, Lord
I'm living out my everyday, ordinary life when thoughts
of discontentment, greed, envy, pride, anger, lust,
discouragement, and a host of other degenerates present
themselves like soldiers reporting for duty—except these
are rogue troops! So, Lord, I'm calling on You to be my
Shield and my protector. I need You to wage war on my
behalf. Take captive this battalion of reprobate thoughts
and make them obedient to Your lordship (2 Corinthians
10:5)!

Thank You that I can run to the strong tower of Your
name and find safety and security within. Amen.

A Star

*"I see him, but not here and now. I perceive him,
but far in the distant future. A star will rise from Jacob;
a scepter will emerge from Israel."*
NUMBERS 24:17 NLT

Lord, on a mission trip to Haiti I visited a village high in the mountains, far removed from any semblance of civilization. We had no clean water. No flushing toilets. No electricity. The darkness of night would fall, heightening the sounds of unfamiliar creatures and distant voodoo ceremonies. Void of city lights, the blackness of our surroundings set me on edge. . .that is, until I looked up. I had never seen anything like it! The utter brilliance of the stars above caught me off guard, taking my breath away.

Jesus, I'm not sure why that memory came rushing into my mind just now—maybe You are reminding me that You're the brilliant light in the midst of this dark world. You shine—undimmed, radiant, and ready to guide. Today, help me to look up. Help me to see the utter brilliance of You, O God, my Star! Amen.

Strength to the Poor and Needy

—⊸⊶⊷—

For thou hast been a strength to the poor,
a strength to the needy in his distress.
Isaiah 25:4 kjv

Jesus, You know what it's like to walk a mile in our shoes. You've felt what we feel and have experienced what we experience. You gave up Your throne for a manger. You traded in Your crown for thorns. You lowered Your position so that mine might be raised. What an inequitable exchange!

Right now I am weak and needy. Right now I call to You—because I know You understand—and I'm begging for the exchange I know You willingly give. Lord, please take this weakness from me and infuse me with Your strength. Let me mount up with wings like eagles. Let me run and not grow weary. I wait for You, O Lord, my Strength. Amen.

A Strong Tower

The name of the LORD is a strong tower;
the righteous man runs into it and is safe.
PROVERBS 18:10 ESV

Strong. Fortified. Available. A tower raised higher than the enemy. A safe haven from the storm. A place of refuge and rest. That is what You are—it is who You are. While I see Your sanctuary towering above the enemy, I also notice tents pitched along the route toward You, each one luring me in with the promise of shelter so readily accessible. But when I enter, I find the walls weak and easily penetrable, no match for the enemy's weapons. Defeat and failure assault me.

O Lord, my Strong Tower, I ask that You remind me to run in Your direction and not give up until I enter into Your presence. Remaining outside is fatal, but dwelling in You ensures safety. Amen.

THE TRUTH

Jesus saith unto him, I am. . .the truth.
JOHN 14:6 KJV

Lord, I desire to have a strong and vigorous faith in You. As Your Word says, "Everyone who has been born of God overcomes the world. And this is the victory that has overcome the world—our faith" (1 John 5:4 ESV).

Lord, I hate to admit this, but You already know— sometimes my faith is so weak. Sometimes doubts creep in. Sometimes Satan, the father of lies, assaults me with his cunning deceptions, and I find myself questioning You. But You have foreseen those times, Lord, and have given me everything I need to stand firm. For You are the Truth, and holding fast to You will bring victory! I ask that Truth flood my mind, protecting me from Satan's fiery arrows. I ask that Truth guard my heart from his attacks. I ask that Truth be the weapon I wield to fight his onslaught!

Thank You for providing all I need to stand firm. Thank You for victory that comes through faith in You. Thank You for being Truth! Amen.

Understanding

〰〰〰

*"Counsel is mine and sound wisdom;
I am understanding, power is mine."*
PROVERBS 8:14 NASB

Lord, I'm confused. Our world is spinning out of control—and I don't know who to trust or how to interpret the circumstances. What used to be called evil is now celebrated as good. What once was up is now down, wrong is right, and wisdom is considered foolishness. The standard has tilted, and societal equilibrium is out of balance. So many voices are shouting against Your truth!

Lord, I need to hear You above the clamor. I beg to be so in tune with Your voice that I hear even Your whisper. Lord of Understanding, infuse me with Your discernment. Speak wisdom to my soul. You say in James that if anyone lacks wisdom he should ask You—and You'll dole it out generously. Lord, I'm asking. Give me wisdom, give me understanding—You are its source. Amen.

THE WAY

⚯

Jesus told him, "I am the way."
JOHN 14:6 HCSB

Jesus, You are the Way—the straight and narrow Way that leads directly to the Father. A thousand other ways stretch before us, broad avenues even, but they lead to destruction. And "there is a way that seems right to a man, but its end is the way to death" (Proverbs 14:12 ESV).

Lord, Satan has many agents highlighting his wicked way, but You, Jesus, are the signpost saying, "This is the way, walk in it" (Isaiah 30:21 ESV).

Help me to walk in Your Way today, Lord Jesus. When other paths present themselves, I pray I will use Your Word as "a lamp to my feet and a light to my path" (Psalm 119:105 ESV). For You have given me a sure Word, Jesus, and I would do well to pay attention to it (2 Peter 1:19 ESV). Amen.

About the Author

LeAnne Blackmore is a veteran Bible teacher, conference speaker, and Bible study author. Her ministry experience runs the gamut from middle school through senior adults, but her heart is for all people to know God by knowing His Word. Currently she is learning to navigate her way through the empty-nest stage of life. If you want to challenge her at ping-pong or Words With Friends, she'll accept—just be prepared for the ruthless competition sure to ensue. LeAnne and her husband, Ron, enjoy traveling, but always love returning home to the beautiful mountains of east Tennessee.

Scripture Index